Proclamation 3

Aids for Interpreting
the Lessons of the Church Year

Advent
Christmas

Bruce Vawter

Elizabeth Achtemeier, series editor

Series A

FORTRESS PRESS Philadelphia

Library of Congress Cataloging in Publication Data

Main entry under title:

Proclamation 3.

　　Consists of 28 volumes in 3 series designated A, B, and C which correspond to the cycles of the three year lectionary. Each series contains 8 basic volumes with the following titles: Advent-Christmas, Epiphany, Lent, Holy Week, Easter, Pentecost 1, Pentecost 2, and Pentecost 3.

　　1. Bible—Homiletical use.　2. Bible—Liturgical lessons, English.　I. Achtemeier, Elizabeth Rice, 1926–　　.

BS534.5.P765　1985　　251　　84–18756
ISBN 0–8006–4106–X (Series B, Pentecost 1)

2563A86　Printed in the United States of America　1–4117

Contents

Series Foreword

Proclamation 3 is an entirely new aid for preaching from the three-year ecumenical lectionary. In outward appearance this new series is similar to *Proclamation: Aids for Interpreting the Lessons of the Church Year* and *Proclamation 2*. But *Proclamation 3* has a new content as well as a new purpose.

First, there is only one author for each of the twenty-eight volumes of *Proclamation 3*. This means that each author handles both the exegesis and the exposition of the stated texts, thus eliminating the possibility of disparity between scholarly apprehension and homiletical application of the appointed lessons. While every effort was made in *Proclamation: Aids* and in *Proclamation 2* to avoid such disparity, it tended to creep in occasionally. *Proclamation 3* corrects that tendency.

Second, *Proclamation 3* is directed primarily at homiletical interpretation of the stated lessons. We have again assembled the finest biblical scholars and preachers available to write for the series; now, however, they bring their skills to us not primarily as exegetes, but as interpreters of the Word of God. Exegetical material is still presented—sometimes at length—but, most important, here it is also applied; the texts are interpreted and expounded homiletically for the church and society of our day. In this new series scholars become preachers. They no longer stand back from the biblical text and just discuss it objectively. The engage it—as the Word of God for the worshiping community. The reader therefore will not find here the divisions between "exegesis" and "homiletical interpretation" that were marked off in the two earlier series. In *Proclamation 3* the work of the pulpit is the context and goal of all that is written.

There is still some slight diversity between the several lections and calendars of the various denominations. In an effort to overcome such diversity, the North American Committee on a Common Lectionary issued an experimental "consensus lectionary" *(The Common Lectionary),* which is now being tried out in some congregations and which will be further altered at the end of a three-year period. When the final form of that lectionary appears, *Proclamation* will take account of it. In the meantime, *Proclamation 3* deals with those texts that are used by *most* denominations on any given Sunday. It also continues to use the Lutheran numbering of the Sundays "after Pentecost." But Episcopalians and Roman Catholics will find most of their stated propers dealt with under this numbering.

Each author writes on three lessons for each Sunday, but no one method of combining the appointed lessons has been imposed upon the writers. The texts are sometimes treated separately, sometimes together—according to the author's own understanding of the texts' relationships and messages. The authors interpret the appointed texts as these texts have spoken to them.

Dr. Bruce Vawter, C.M., is a Roman Catholic priest, currently chairman and professor in the Religious Studies Department of De Paul University, Chicago. He is the author of many books in the biblical field and has contributed numerous articles to scholarly and popular journals, as well as to the previous editions of the *Proclamation* series.

The First Sunday in Advent

Lutheran	Roman Catholic	Episcopal	Pres/UCC/Chr	Meth/COCU
Isa. 2:1–5	Isa. 2:1–5	Isa. 2:1–5	Isa. 2:1–5	Isa. 2:1–5
Rom. 13:11–14	Rom. 13:11–14	Rom. 13:8–14	Rom. 13:11–14	Rom. 13:8–14
Matt. 24:37–44 or Matt. 21:1–11	Matt. 24:37–44	Matt. 24:36–44	Matt. 24:37–44	Matt. 24:36–44

FIRST LESSON: ISAIAH 2:1–5

Our first reading today consists of a passage that is also found in Mic. 4:1–3, trivial differences aside. There is no point in enquiring about authorship: these verses, a piece of song or poetry, probably liturgical in origin, have been inserted into the books of Isaiah and Micah at a time much later than either of these prophets of the eighth century B.C. They celebrate the destiny of the holy city Jerusalem to be a wellspring of religious truth and teaching for all the nations of the earth. Practically all their language, though in part it exploits some older themes, testifies to their genesis in Israel's postexilic age. The "latter days" of which they speak are doubtless those times-beyond-present-history to which Ezek. 38:16 looks, the age in which God will call for a settling of accounts, ordaining salvation for his faithful people and requiting the sins of the wicked—the age dreamed of by the apocalyptists, in other words.

Yet this is hardly an apocalyptic vision in the usual sense of the word. Here there is no triumphalism of a vindicated Israel rejoicing in the humbling of its enemies. God is exalted, surely, precisely as he had revealed himself to Israel. But the "nations" figure not as evil forces to be overcome, rather, as equals to be absorbed as coreligionists. Mount Zion shall be exalted not for its own sake nor for the sake of Israel, but rather that it become a beacon to attract the whole world to *torah,* the word of God.

This is the doctrine of the Third rather than of the Second Isaiah (cf. Isa. 66:18–23), the doctrine as well of other postexilic authors such as those responsible for the books of Malachi, Jonah, and Ruth.

7

It is one of the Old Testament's highest achievements, the inspired utterance of a poet who has seen to the full the purpose God had in choosing Israel for his special people and in establishing Jerusalem and its temple for the special place of his presence. His purpose entails nothing less than the salvation of all people through Israel and through the revelation found in Israel's history.

This vision of God's purposes is not complete: we are not yet in the New Testament when it will be proclaimed that in Christ Jesus "there is neither Jew nor Greek, neither slave nor free, neither male nor female" (Gal. 3:28). Its universalism is one of Jewish proselytism: the Gentiles are acceptable to God, surely, but only if they trade in their cultural values for Jewish currency. But we do well to reflect on this universalism not as it was first historically conditioned, but as it eventually became in the fullness of time when the seed sown by prophetic words like these had borne fruit. And we also do well to ask ourselves to what extent we remain at the beginning rather than share in the conclusion of such a prophetic process.

The mind-set that identifies the revealed word with the cultural circumstances and limitations that first attended it has been no monopoly of Judaism. Paul encountered it in the Galatian church, and patristic sources testify that it persisted well into early Christian times. It remains among us in some notable examples, and in others that are not so readily noted. How often has Christianity been confused—and by Christians themselves—with "Western civilization"? How often have the social and moral values of a class or of a given era been assumed to be integral to the handing on of the gospel rather than part of the dispensable baggage the church has picked up along the way?

"In a higher world it is otherwise," wrote John Henry Newman, "but here below to live is to change, and to be perfect is to have changed often." To recognize that new problems require new answers, that the social, political, or other aspirations of Christian men and women today are not necessarily met by responses that were satisfactory to their grandparents, is not to compromise or to betray the gospel. It is, rather, to respond to the challenge of the liberating Word of God.

SECOND LESSON: ROMANS 13:11–14

The Epistle and the Gospel readings for this day are thematically connected and well adapted to this beginning of the Advent season.

Both are concerned with the *parousia,* the final coming of the Lord and the consummation of God's plan for humankind on earth, a consummation that had its proximate beginning in his coming in the manifestation of the mystery of the incarnation. Both passages are fraught with a spirit of expectation.

Paul, in this situation of expectation, emphasizes the need of preparedness. Unlike his vagueness about times and seasons in 1 Thess. 5:1–11, a passage otherwise remarkably parallel to this one of Romans, here he says that the "hour" of the Lord's coming is known. This is the *kairos,* the moment of decision and destiny. It is impossible to avoid the conclusion that Paul's injunctions were colored by an assumption that the end was very near. The salvation he is imminently expecting is, as always in the Pauline vocabulary, eschatological salvation consummated in the resurrection. The same assumption colors many other Pauline exhortations without, however, affecting their validity and continuing relevance. For those who believe, the *kairos* is always at hand, for faith is the beginning and condition of a work of God whose destined fulfillment is salvation. The air of urgency we sense in these lines is not dispelled, therefore, by what would later be called the "delay" of the *parousia.*

To describe these final days which are the era of the church, Paul resorts to apocalyptic language. From the contemporary Qumran literature we are familiar with the eschatological battle to be waged between "the children of light" and "the children of darkness." Darkness is the world of the unredeemed, the unregenerate. Light is the world of God's enlightenment, the world of faith and the way of salvation. Darkness pertains to the night, the time for sleeping. Hence it behooves those who have come into God's light to awake from sleep, now that the day has come. They must put aside the works of darkness, all that was characteristic of their unregenerate past, and put on the armor of light. What that armor is Paul details in 1 Thess. 5:8: the breastplate of faith and love, and the helmet of the hope of salvation. These "theological virtues" of faith, hope, and charity appear here as defensive weapons against relapse into the old ways which the apostle stigmatizes by appending one of his typical catalogues of vices.

It is not merely with defensive armor, however, that the believer is to go forward to face his destiny. It is not only that he must make no provision for the flesh. "Flesh" for Paul is in the same bracket with "darkness": it is the human person still enslaved to sin, not merely to sexual sin (the "debauchery" of Paul's list) but to every kind of sinful conduct for which the unregenerate self has a desire. He must also "put on the Lord Jesus Christ" (cf. Gal. 3:27). This is a very active, positive engagement contracted in the Christian calling. One does not resist evil simply by not giving in to it. To sustain Paul's metaphor, one does not arm a warrior only that he remain unharmed on the field of battle. To put on Christ is to be "in Christ" and "in the Spirit": for all practical purposes the two expressions are synonymous. To be in Christ is to be *alive* to God (Rom. 6:11), to participate in the Spirit (Phil. 2:1). And the fruit of the Spirit is love, joy, peace, patience, kindness, goodness, faithfulness, gentleness, and self-control (Gal. 5:22). All these flow from the faith, hope, and love that are the response to God's summons to salvation.

GOSPEL: MATTHEW 24:37–44

The Gospel reading for today is part of the last of the five great discourses into which Matthew has distributed the sayings of Jesus. The eschatological discourse of Matthew 24—25 represents a considerable enlargement over Mark 13, which it has substantially followed up to this point, and the verses we have here are part of that enlargement. Since they also appear in Luke 17:26–27, 34–35 (though in a different context, as a response to the Pharisees rather than an instruction given to the disciples, and with a different application), they evidently derive from that non-Markan source upon which Matthew and Luke have drawn independently and which partly accounts for the Synoptic phenomenon.

The feature of the *parousia* most stressed by the Gospel writers is its sudden and unpredictable coming. A further complication is caused by the mixing of this feature of the *parousia* with another, less definitive visitation of God recognized to have taken place in the destruction of the Jerusalem temple by the Romans in A.D. 70. The two events are not brought together by Luke, but they are by Matthew and they already had been by Mark. This fact is undoubtedly accounted for by the early Christian persuasion of the nearness of the end time, a persuasion seemingly confirmed by the passing away of God's holy city and the temple of his presence. In any case, the Gospel itself serves as precedent for the church's liturgical use of these eschatological sayings to refer to other comings of the Lord, such as the one for which we are preparing.

The unexpectedness of God's visitation in the coming of the Son of Man is first underscored by evoking the Genesis story of Noah and the flood. It is interesting to contrast Matthew's conception of the flood generation with that of some Jewish legends doubtless known to him. The rabbinical authors of the legends took Gen. 6:12 very, very seriously: not only was the earth filled with violence and humankind vile, but *"all flesh* had corrupted their way upon the earth." For them this meant that every kind of enormity was being committed by all the members of the animal kingdom, dogs breeding with wolves, roosters with peacocks, and the like. They tried to outdo one another in imagining the many variations on the theme of depravity that had been introduced into a world that God had once pronounced good.

The Gospel wastes no time on such speculations. It is not interested in offering reasons for God's intervention with the flood but rather in citing the flood as a disaster unprovided for. Hence, the people of the time of the flood are described merely as eating and drinking, marrying and giving in marriage—going about the ordinary routine of human existence, in other words. This matter-of-fact approach to the cautionary example of the flood is surely more effective in exhorting Christians to vigilance than is a rehearsal of the human potential for sinning. It is not only the wicked who will be caught unawares when the Son of Man comes. Nor are these words being addressed to the wicked to call them to mend their ways. What is being stressed at present is not so much moral preparedness as it is psychological preparedness. That is to say, in God's own time will come what God has promised, and it will come surely and unpredictably. Words such as these, then, are fittingly directed to believers of any time who may be tempted to think that, since God has not yet acted when and as they think he should, they may therefore have complacent recourse to a reciprocal inaction. Whether it is a *parousia* that has lost its urgency because it has not adjusted to a supposed timetable, or some other response that God was expected to accord with human expectations, the answer is the same: be vigilant in expecting the unexpected.

There is really no conflict, or at best only a slight conflict, in emphasis between what is said here and what appear above in this same chapter as "signs" of an imminent *parousia* described in traditional apocalyptic language. These "signs" are not so much portents of the *parousia* as they are part and parcel with the *parousia* itself, apocalyptically conceived. Neither in Matthew nor in Mark does Jesus actually satisfy the curiosity of the disciples on "the sign of your coming and of the close of the age."

The little parables that follow continue and illustrate what has been said about the necessity of vigilance and awareness of the right priorities. Two men will be in the field, going about their day-by-day routine like the men and women before the flood. Only one will be ready for the Lord's coming and thus "taken." To all outward appearances these two will be of the same condition, but God will recognize his own. Similarly the two women grinding at the communal mill. The householder who is graced by an accommodating thief with the schedule set for the break-in will of course be on guard precisely at that time. Readiness to meet the Lord would likewise be a matter of ease and leisure were the moment of his coming capable of advance notice. Then constant vigilance would not be a necessity. But as it is, constant vigilance in the face of the inexorability of a rendering of accounts whose time cannot be predicted is the guarantor of responsible living of the Christian life.

Since we cannot count on a tranquil deathbed on which to enact our conversion, since there is no assurance of a sufficiency of time between the saddle and the ground, we are constrained to live every moment as though it were our last and there could be no other. The faithful Christian who lives every moment as though it were the last can be certain of having lived a Christian life at every moment.

The Second Sunday in Advent

Lutheran	Roman Catholic	Episcopal	Pres/UCC/Chr	Meth/COCU
Isa. 11:1–10	Isa. 11:1–10	Isa. 11:1–10	Isa. 11:1–10	Isa. 11:1–10
Rom. 15:4–13	Rom. 15:4–9	Rom. 15:4–13	Rom. 15:4–9	Rom. 15:4–13
Matt. 3:1–12	Matt. 3:1–12	Matt. 3:1–12	Matt. 3:1–12	Matt. 3:1–12

FIRST LESSON: ISAIAH 11:1–10

This passage, plainly messianic in inspiration, looks forward to the coming, in God's providence, of an ideal king of Davidic ancestry who will not only continue and fulfill God's intentions for the good of his people Israel but will also be one in whom the nations of the earth will rejoice. The church has applied this text to the Lord Jesus Christ and in commemoration of his nativity not by a mere appropriation of language but in virtue of a historical typology that presupposes a continuity of revelation.

It is also fitting that the passage should be part of the book of Isaiah, where it forms a conclusion to the so-called Book of Immanuel. Isaiah, alone of all the preexilic prophets of Israel, made the fortunes of the Davidic dynasty and its relation to God's plan for his people one of the major emphases of his prophetic career. However, a closer look at our passage will indicate not only that it is not a unity but also the unlikelihood of its having come to us directly from the eighth-century Isaiah.

There is a tension between vv. 6–9, another of those idyllic portrayals of the eschatological future when nothing short of the ideal shall exist in God's renewed world, and vv. 1–5 and 10, where the messianic king very much has to struggle to make justice prevail in this world. Furthermore, there are in vv. 6–9 echoes of themes and the language (Isa. 65:25 and Hab. 2:14, for example) that pertain to a time later than Isaiah's. But even vv. 1–5 and 10, which describe the messianic king, seem to presuppose circumstances far different from those of Isaiah's era. The reference to a "stump" of the tree of Jesse from which a new "branch" is expected fits better the historical situation of postexilic prophets like Haggai (2:20–23) and Zechariah (4:1–7; 6:9–14). These prophets, too, were looking for a fulfillment of the destiny God had assigned to the house of David, no longer from the direct line of descent, which had been terminated by the exile and disruption of 587–586 B.C., yet still from one who could rightly be acclaimed a Davidic descendant.

These critical observations are necessary if we are to be properly situated historically in respect to this reading, but of course they do not affect its essential message nor the relevance of our celebration of it today. It does indeed refer to a coming messianic king who will be God's instrument to bring about universal salvation and peace. Such was an ideal expressed by many anonymous prophets in vision conditioned by their time, and such is the ideal perceived by us in vision conditioned by our time.

The description of the messianic king in vv. 2–5 is interesting for numerous reasons, not the least of which is its very typically Israelite mingling and adaptation of motifs that had been borrowed from other cultures. This is a feature that underlines the universalism of the passage.

In vv. 2–3a we have typical "wisdom" language. The tradition responsible for the wisdom writings of the Old Testament was a venerable one, international in its origins, ecumenical in its religious language. It was not unreligious; rather, it adapted to the religion of whatever culture it took root in. Here, in an Israelite text, wisdom is ascribed to "the spirit of the Lord." It is also said that the king's delight will be in the fear of the Lord, echoing one of the favorite aphorisms of Israel's wisdom, that its beginning is in "the fear of the Lord" (Prov. 1:7 and repeatedly thereafter). But neither was religion its origin. Wisdom, counsel, understanding, knowledge—all these part of the technical terminology of the wisdom schools—were first thought of as the product of observation, reflection, meditation upon experience, and applied common sense (cf. Prov. 1:2–6). In other words, wisdom, when it was put in service to the contemplation of sacred things, constituted a kind of "natural theology" which, far from being a rival to the word of divine revelation, served to confirm it as in accord with human reasoning, which is also the gift of God.

The second part of the description of the messianic king, vv. 3b–5, is an Israelite adaptation of the kingly ideal that was the common property of the many cultures of the ancient Near East. In this ideal conception of what it was to be a king, it was agreed that he should embody the divine quality of *ṣedeq*, "justice" or "righteousness," that which would make him immune to blandishments, special pleading, sentimentality, and the false mercy of permissiveness, and enable him to govern in a God-like way, with strict and evenhanded justice bestowed on good and bad alike. This was obviously a highly religious concept. It explains the divine or at least semidivine qualities and titles accorded the king in ancient Near Eastern societies, Israel's own not excepted. Such are the ideals, however imperfectly they may be realized at times, that nourish the spirit of hope.

The picture of vv. 6–8 is one of "paradise regained." In the Genesis story of the earthly paradise there was a complete harmony of man with nature and of nature with itself internally. Now, in the messianic kingdom to come, that harmony will be restored, with peace replacing violence, with natural rivalries and predations abolished. All this is symbolism, of course, just as the Genesis story was one of symbolism. But the gap between mythical and matter-of-fact is firmly bridged in

v. 9: paradise will be this solid earth filled with "knowledge of the Lord." Such knowledge is neither esoteric nor mystical; it is righteous conduct acknowledging the moral will of God (cf. Hos. 4:1–2).

In v. 10 the messianic king, it is said, will be an "ensign" to the nations of the earth. This repeats an idea expressed often in the book of Isaiah (v. 12; also 18:3; 49:22; 62:10). He will be hailed as a universal savior, this one who is the fulfillment of Israel's kingly ideal.

SECOND LESSON: ROMANS 15:4–13

This reading is part of a passage in which Paul exhorts his readers to harmony and mutual forbearance, holding up Christ himself as the model for their conduct. It is possible, though by no means certain, that the tensions in the Roman church that provided the occasion for his exhortation were those that rose between Christians of Jewish and Gentile backgrounds, in which case Paul has made a clever use of the Jewish circumstances of Jesus' descent and ministry contrasted with the universal implications of his gospel. Whether or not Jewish-Gentile tension was present in the minds of the Romans, it was always a concern in Paul's mind, and he was ever at pains to resolve it in the light of the eternal designs of God. Thus we have here yet another instance of how the apostle reconciled the Jewishness of Jesus (and of himself) with his personal mission to the Gentiles—which was in turn only his part in the larger mission of a church that was more and more outgrowing its Jewish origins and becoming increasingly Gentile.

Although Paul holds up Jesus as a model for emulation, he has made only a fleeting reference to his model in the preceding v. 3. "Christ did not please himself," five words in English, four in Greek, is Paul's laconic summation here of the theology of the great christological hymn of Phil. 2:5–11. Instead of a rehearsal of events in the life of Jesus he begins a series of scriptural citations. This manner of procedure is typically Pauline. In contrast with modern-day Christians like ourselves who are both confident of our ability to reconstruct the past and place great emphasis on the importance of doing so, Paul evinces very little interest in Christ "according to the flesh" (Rom. 9:5)—the historical Jesus—despite the fact that he was obviously in a far better position than we to be put in contact with the "brute facts" that lie behind the theology of the Gospels. This lack of curiosity reflects his mistrust of "the wisdom of man" which can get in the way of the Word of God, to prevent it being heard clearly. Always Paul prefers the sure ground of Scripture, convinced that all has been written to the end that the gospel may be seen as a sure basis for hope.

The harmony to which Paul exhorts the Romans is thus motivated by the lack of self-seeking the Scripture attributes to Christ in his saving work. In view of this background it is possible to see that more is meant in conclusion than simply that the Romans should offer a more unified presence unto God and praise him with one voice. Paul uses the expression: the God *and* Father of our Lord Jesus Christ. He is the God of Jesus as he is the God of us all: he is our creator. He is the Father of Christ, however, in a way unique: he is the one who sent his only Son into the world for our redemption.

The conclusion of this exhortation explains why it was that Jesus the Jew should have become the Savior of Gentiles. He was born a Jew that he might show forth the fidelity of God to his promises: it was with Abraham that God first covenanted, with him and his descendants, and thus it was within the divine plan that salvation should come from the Jews (John 4:22). But this salvation was intended for the Gentiles as well, in proof of which are cited Ps. 18:49; Deut. 32:43; Ps. 117:1, and the Isa. 11:10 of our first reading. Paul does not, of course, justify his reading of these texts on any grounds of historical criticism. Neither, however, is he simply appropriating their language to purposes alien to their meaning. He confidently reads the Old Testament as though it were a Christian book in virtue of his conviction that "whatever was written in former days was written for our instruction" and because of his belief that Christ is the key to the Scriptures. Anyone who can accept in principle that the Bible is a unity, Old Testament and New, should be able to follow Paul in his argument, even though present-day exegetical method and presuppositions are rather different from Paul's.

It is worthy of note that Paul—along with the other New Testament authors—finds it a convenience to his argument to refer to the ancient Greek translation of the Old Testament rather than to the Hebrew original. This Greek version, the Septuagint, had translated not only the Hebrew Bible but also some other works of a sacred character which were not finally accepted into the Jewish canon of Scripture. It was a work produced by Jews of the Diaspora in Alexandria at various times during the first two and a half centuries before Christ, and it was intended for Jews—now in the great majority—who no longer understood Hebrew and needed a Bible in their own idiom. The Septuagint was the first biblical translation, and every subsequent translator through the ages has been in debt to it. But the Septuagint is not always mere translation. Sometimes, and deliberately so, it represents a transformation of the biblical word, testifying to the development of thought that had taken place within the faith community where the word continued to live and to vitalize. It was the Septuagint that became the Old Testament of early Christianity, as it remains the Old Testament of the churches of the East. As just noted, it is, with only minor exceptions, the Old Testament that is cited in the New Testament. Paul's use of it here is significant in view of the role it played in bridging the chasm of separation between Jew and Gentile and of making possible that enlargement of the mission of Jesus with which the apostle is concerned in this passage.

GOSPEL: MATTHEW 3:1–12

All of the Gospels are in agreement in putting the ministry of John the Baptist in close association with that of Jesus, though they tend each to treat that association somewhat differently, and in particular they interpret differently the baptism Jesus was known to have received at the Baptist's hands. Here we are concerned only with the preaching of John in the wilderness of Judea and his identification of himself as Jesus' precursor.

All three of the Synoptic Gospels characterize the appearance of the Baptist as the fulfillment of the words of Isa. 40:3, at the beginning of the Book of Consolation of the Second Isaiah which proclaims "glad tidings" (Isa. 40:9), prototype of the good news of the gospel. As herald of this good news, the coming of the kingdom of God foreshadowed in our first reading—"kingdom of heaven" is Matthew's habitual paraphrase, in keeping with the Jewish practice of avoiding the use of the divine name—John's message is one of repentance in preparation. In the Greek of the Gospel "repentance" *(metanoia)* is, literally, a change of mind or disposition, a conversion. It means something very positive, not merely a sorrow or regret for past wrongdoing, but an entire change of posture which is not only a preparation for the coming of God's kingdom but is also in a very true sense its beginning, its taking hold of the individual person. The Old Testament idea underlying the biblical Greek is the prophets' call to "return," a word especially favored by Jeremiah, implying a resumption of one's covenant commitments.

In addition to his being the herald foretold by Isaiah, John the Baptist is seen by Matthew in v. 4 as a second Elijah the prophet (cf. 2 Kings 1:8). In Jewish eschatological speculation the figure of Elijah was assigned various roles, including the one that is accorded him in Mal. 4:5–5 (RSV enumeration), to be a reconciler and restorer of Israel before the final judgment day (see also Sir. 48:10). Reconciliation is indeed the message of John's call to repentance, despite the harsh words that follow immediately in Matthew and Luke.

Both Matthew and Luke have inserted at this point invectives that the Baptist hurls against those whom we are probably supposed to view as representing the religious "establishment" which will shortly be found in bitter opposition to the preaching of Jesus. This is clearer in Matthew's account that it is in Luke's, for while the latter speaks simply of the "multitudes" that had come out to hear John's words, Matthew specifies that it was "the Pharisees and Sadducees" who were the target of his wrath. Also, Luke goes on to show that among these "multitudes" were many of apparent good will, who desired only further instruction about the repentance expected of them. The purpose of these verses, besides foreshadowing the obduracy with which the call to conversion will often be met, is doubtless to serve as a reminder of the substantial difference that existed between the kingdom of God proclaimed by John and Jesus and the kingdom of God of popular expectation.

The good news is a new good, a good that does not respect inherited privilege nor confine itself to what is safe, comfortable, and familiar. The figure of the barren tree or the tree that no longer bears good fruit is frequent in the Bible. It will be cut down, that tree. Other children of Abraham will arise to replace those found unworthy of the same. The coming of the kingdom will be a tragic response to the misplaced hope of many who have awaited it in complacent confidence.

The Baptist's contrast of his baptism and of himself with the baptism and person of the one "who is coming" is strongly reminiscent of our first reading today, the Isaian text about the messianic king. He will be, says John, a mightier one: one who will possess the spirit of counsel and might as foretold by the prophet. And he will baptize not with water alone but with the Holy Spirit, the bestower of wisdom and understanding, knowledge and the fear of the Lord. John also adds "fire," a time-honored symbol of the divine presence. This presence will be one of discernment and judgment, the Baptist makes clear, with a final change of metaphor. The coming one will be like a thresher who separates the good grain from the chaff. His coming will be for decision, and for the judgment that follows on decision.

The Third Sunday in Advent

Lutheran	Roman Catholic	Episcopal	Pres/UCC/Chr	Meth/COCU
Isa. 35:1–10	Isa. 35:1–6a, 10	Isa. 35:1–10	Isa. 35:1–6a, 10	Isa. 35:1–10
James 5:7–10	James 5:7–10	James 5:7–10	James 5:7–10	James 5:7–10
Matt. 11:2–11	Matt. 11:2–11	Matt. 11:2–11	Matt. 11:2–11	Matt. 11:2–11

FIRST LESSON: ISAIAH 35:1–10

This beautiful, almost lyrical chapter of the book of Isaiah has rather evidently been inspired by the Book of the Consolation of Israel which begins at Isa. 40:1. It employs much of the same language and many of the same themes and images. However, there is also an important difference. No longer is the purview limited to the return from the Babylonian captivity. Instead, the author seems to contemplate an ingathering of exiles from wherever they may be found. This, then, is the vision of Isa. 27:12–13, a vision dependent on, but probably rather later than, the good news proclaimed by the Second Isaiah.

It is doubtless in order to remind ourselves that from the standpoint of strictly literal fulfillment, what the prophet looked forward to was never actually to be. Before the exile was yet over, both Jeremiah (e.g., in chap. 31 of his book) and Ezekiel (frequently, but most graphically in the images of chap. 37) had enthusiastically looked forward to a restoration of the whole of Israel, Israel north and Judah south, a reconstitution of the people from the remnants not only of those who had been carried off by the Chaldeans to exile in Babylon, but also of those who had been scattered abroad by the Assyrians and other conquerors of the past. This theme was taken up by subsequent prophets and by many who supplemented the prophetic collections.

However, it was an expectation never to be realized, not within the time of the historical Israel. Whoever would look for prophetic fulfillment in passages like this, therefore, must find it in the spiritual sense in which we are now taking it, wherein the church recognizes its Old Testament roots.

The imagery of the passage is exuberant without being extravagant or relying upon apocalyptic. The picture of a desert brought to bloom with the lushness of the Lebanon, of Mount Carmel, and of the Sharon valley, had of course a greater impact for people more conscious of the terrors of the surrounding wilderness than are most of us today. Paradoxically, at least some of those places whose proverbial beauty the author contrasts with the desert are in these times of ours little better than desert themselves. For the most part, this sad state of affairs is due to human irresponsibility, abdication of the stewardship of the world and its resources with which God once charged humankind.

When we come to the Gospel reading for today, we will see how this Isaian text had, already in New Testament times, been perceived as a mirror of the messianic era: when the blind shall see, the deaf shall hear, the lame shall walk, and the dumb shall speak. The banishment of physical evil as a sign of the breaking of the bonds of spiritual and moral evil—the coming in of the kingdom of God heralded by miracles of healing—was perhaps more easily appreciated in biblical times than it is in our own. We have means of alleviating physical distress and coping with handicaps that were then unknown. On the other hand, however, it is precisely in our times that we have been rendered more and more sensitive to a holistic perception of human existence, to the intimate connection that exists between the spiritual well-being of human society and the quality of its physical life. Such a sensitivity is altogether in keeping with the biblical view of the human person, which saw it as a whole and not rigidly compartmentalized into the spiritual and the material. (As has frequently been pointed out, the biblical concept of "spirit," life-giving and life-sustaining breath, itself begins as a "material" term.) The same biblical understanding is warrant for a perception of the church's mission to further the consummation of God's kingdom that does not limit it to "saving souls" and declare off limits efforts to alleviate social and economic misery and inequities. The church, itself a society, is sent into the world not as to a mass of discrete individuals but as to a social entity out of which the kingdom is to be formed.

Nor may we fudge the issue by thinking to measure our service to humankind, the potential kingdom of God, in direct proportion to the kingdom's coming, following a timetable of our own devising. It does no good to preach the gospel to a starving man, and there is something obscene about our requiring that he hear our preaching as the price of our feeding him. For a great number of men and women, perhaps for the great majority, the best that is to be hoped from the church's ministry today is simply some help enabling them to live as human beings and not as animals, some hope of a life without fear and violence and subhuman filth and poverty. Indeed, at times the best that the church can offer is the opportunity to die with dignity. Such must be our recognition of things as they are, since societies can be every bit as sick as the individuals who make up societies.

Christians sometimes look askance at the materialist imagery with which the Old Testament surrounds its descriptions of the good life, even the good eschatological life. We have already suggested that the Old Testament's analysis of human existence, its approach to the person according to the well-known formula of "animated body" rather than in the Greek way of a soul imprisoned in flesh, may have a great deal to say to us in our attempts to comprehend the nature of human beings. Thus far human being in the abstract. Perhaps we can venture further. Perhaps the "materialism" of the Old Testament may have even more to say to us when today we would approach our fellow human beings not as abstractions but in the concrete circumstances of their lives.

Our passage concludes with further images of the transformation of the desert from a place of terror and inhospitable foreboding into a smooth highway for the Lord's coming and an earthly paradise. Abundance of water was a poignant symbol of beneficence and well-being in the water-thirsty lands of the Near East. In the vision of Ezek. 47:1–12 there is a sustained exploitation of this same theme, when water is seen flowing from beneath the threshold of the restored temple toward the east, deep and pure water which fructifies the new Israel and turns the salt sea into a garden spot, literally bringing forth life from death. The symbolism is hardly less meaningful today.

It is not beside the point, too, in view of what anthropological studies have done to add to our understanding of humankind's literary history, to reflect on the sure instinct that prompted the ancient creation myths to seek the origins of life in the earth's primordial waters.

SECOND LESSON: JAMES 5:7–10

The Epistle of James is not everybody's favorite portion of the New Testament. Luther's opinion of it as an "epistle of straw" is well known. But even without necessarily sharing the view of the great reformer—who in this instance was not above some rather arbitrary and peremptory judgments to sustain that view—one is permitted to wonder how many would agree with a recent commentator (Peter H. Davids) whose first words are: "The Epistle of James is one of the most exciting parts of the New Testament." Solid, yes. Sensible, down-to-earth, invaluable counsel and instruction—all of that. But exciting?

Nevertheless, it would be a pity were there more nay- than yea-sayers to that proposition, for the Epistle of James *is* exciting, in many ways. One way that becomes immediately evident in this pericope is the positive side of what was once thought to be a decisively negative verdict on the writing. We may find it strange that at one time even some respected critics claimed that this was not at first a Christian work at all, but merely a Jewish homiletical tract that had been superficially adapted to a Christian audience. Strange, since such a judgment itself had to rest on the crudest kind of superficiality, straining at gnats and swallowing camels whole. If the name of Jesus shows up only twice in the letter—and admittedly these could have been interpolations, if it had happened that way—still, the attentive readers should have no trouble recognizing that James is often speaking of Jesus and sometimes quoting him. The work is Christian through and through, but this is a familiar letter and not a treatise, intended not for an uninformed public but for brothers and sisters in the faith (1:2) who doubtless knew about as much of the words and deeds of Jesus as James did.

The positive side of all this is that our attention has been drawn to the undeniable fact that the Epistle of James is, for all of its Christian character, also very Jewish. It is Jewish not simply because it is an "epistle to the Hebrews," addressed to "the twelve tribes in the Dispersion" (1:1)—whether this means that its intended readers were exclusively Jewish Christians is not certain, and immaterial. It is Jewish because it is redolent of the air that was breathed in the very earliest days of apostolic Christianity. If we would have an idea of what the synagogue sermons of Jesus sounded like, or his and his first disciples' preaching in Galilee and Judea, we need seek no further than this Epistle of James. The proof of that is to be found in one of the major emphases of this writing, which also forms the immediate context of today's reading.

In the New Testament, diatribes against the rich are uttered only by Jesus and James (Luke 6:24–25; James 5:1–6). Jesus and James alone single out the poor as belonging to the kingdom of God (Luke 6:20–21; James 2:5). Jesus, particularly as he is presented by the Gospel of Luke but also elsewhere, James and the *Shepherd of Hermas,* one of the noncanonical works of Christian antiquity, testify that the Old Testament prophetic ideal of the ʿ*anawim,* the righteous poor, was very much alive among the people from whose midst the church was born. It is these poor to whom James has addressed his letter, and it is these poor whom he is exhorting to patience in the passage we are reading today.

Those to whom James was speaking were expecting an imminent *parousia,* and James shows that he shared that expectation: "The coming of the Lord is at hand." However, the patience to which he called them (*makrothymia,* "endurance") was not in view of a coming that had been "delayed" in their eyes. James's emphasis was not upon the nearness of the *parousia,* to reassure those who were impatient in their waiting, but on the fact and significance of the *parousia:* judgment day coming, vindication of the just, casting down of the wicked. These were people suffering persecution and discrimination, for whom the imminent coming of the Lord was the hope that could sustain the endurance of their bitter lot.

This was no "pie in the sky" pablum being dispensed by James, as Christian preachers are said to have dispensed it to slaves laboring on southern plantations. No one who has read James's epistle through will be under any doubt about that. But for Christians the Lord is the only ultimate judge, and meanwhile what cannot be cured must be endured.

James's injunction to patience is accompanied by a little parable taken from the Palestinian scene. The Palestinian farmer must indeed be a model of patience, for from the grudging soil of his land he cannot expect the bounty on which his life depends until it has been watered by both the autumn and the spring rains. The expression "The early and the late (rain)" is familiar from the Old Testament (Hos. 6:3; Jer. 5:24; etc.), so much so that in the best manuscript tradition of the

Epistle of James the Greek word for "rain" does not even occur but is understood. Some other manuscripts, good ones for that matter, have misunderstood the expression and repeated the word "fruit" to go with it. An incidental point, perhaps, but it does show that James knew his Old Testament and his Palestine as some later Christian scribes did not. RSV's "establish your hearts" is an unnecessarily wooden translation of a Semitism. It is another Old Testament saying, enjoining courage and resolution of purpose in the face of adversity and the perilous unknown. In 4:14 James had already reminded his readers that they could not know what tomorrow might bring.

Some critics find v. 9 somewhat out of place here, better suited to be a conclusion to 4:11–12 above, where the talk was about fraternal harmony and forbearance, rather than serving as an apparent interruption in this little discourse on patience. But given the informal and homiletical style of the author, we are probably out of order if we try to rearrange this. Furthermore, it might be thought that this seeming aside actually fits the context psychologically. It is not pretty, but it is a fact of human nature that a common misery or repression or stress that ought to unite people and bring them together often works to just the opposite effect, encouraging envy, self-seeking, and mutual recriminations. The poor know best of all that poverty does not ennoble anyone.

James's final words, using the prophets as examples of the longsuffering and patience of which he has been speaking, have also disturbed some readers who think that a truly Christian author should have proposed Jesus himself as the example and model. Such an objection seems frivolous. That prophets were already well established in the popular mind as martyrs to the cause of truth, and to invoke their memory in this connection was almost inevitable—in Matt. 5:12, in fact, this is done by the Lord himself. Besides, we are engaged with examples of patient endurance while waiting on the Lord's coming, and to this end the prophets serve very nicely while the Lord does not.

We should not conclude this reading without asking ourselves to what extent we may presume to associate ourselves with the recipients of James's letter. These people, these first Christians, were far from being the respectable members and pillars of society we like to see fill our churches on Sundays. If truth were told, we would probably be rather embarrassed if they sought entrance to our churches, and for their part they would probably find us more identifiable with their oppressors than with themselves.

It is true that the prophetic ideal of the *'anawim* is not some simple-minded equation of poverty with righteousness and affluence with wickedness. The idealization of the poor grew out of their oppression by the powerful and their confident reliance on the Lord for redress. James, too, does not excoriate the rich except that they continue the evil history of oppression and the abuse of power (2:6–7). We do not consciously belong to this history. Why, then, might the poor count us among their oppressors?

The prophets can answer this question for us. When Amos was defending the just poor against those who lived at ease and were complacent (6:1), or those whom he called the fat Bashan cows of Samaria (4:1), or when Isaiah vented his sarcasm on the haughty daughters of Zion (4:16), they were speaking to the indifferent, to those who did not want to know the world in which they lived. As these lines are being written, there is news from one of our more pleasant cities of the demolition there of the "troll villages," the shantytowns of mattresses and cardboard boxes used by the homeless to shelter under bridges, and of the covering over of sidewalk heat ventilators sought out by street people against the winter cold. Out of sight, out of mind. They also oppress the poor who declare that they do not exist.

GOSPEL: MATTHEW 11:2–11

This episode involving John the Baptist, some of his disciples, and Jesus is related by both Matthew and Luke from their common non-Markan source. Luke has expanded on the source to some degree in setting the scene, probably simply in the interests of good narration, but it may be doubted that he has really improved upon it. The place of the story in Matthew's Gospel is significant for its interpretation. It is part of the narrative introduction to the third of the great discourses into which Matthew has distributed the major emphases of Jesus's teaching, which in this instance take the form of the parables of the kingdom. It is the nature of the kingdom and its paradoxes that are at issue in this section, and confrontation with these issues begins in this story.

The question has been raised whether it was the evangelist's intention to picture John the Baptist himself in a quandary over Jesus' messianic character. Or was John sending his disciples just that they might be reassured? Taking the passage for the instructional instrument that it is, it is safe to say that its whole tenor, and especially its conclusion, makes good sense only on the assumption that the Baptist himself had a problem for which he was seeking a solution. That he should have sent disciples rather than come personally is explained for Matthew by the fact that he was in prison and therefore restricted in his movements.

This episode speaks to only one aspect of a "John-the-Baptist question" that troubled the earliest Christian writers in various ways and provoked them into offering diverse accountings of a relationship that was known to have existed but whose memory had become somewhat cloudy. The Baptist and Jesus had been associated at the time the kingdom first began to be proclaimed by both. That was one inescapable datum. The association, in the gospel tradition, had come to be explained as that of a self-confessed precursor who deferred to another greater than he; this we have seen in our previous reading. And still the problem remained. Now that John was dead, his influence lived on in disciples who did not confess Jesus and who, possibly, had never even heard of him (cf. Matt. 9:14; Acts 19:1–7). How was this situation to be reconciled with the Christian belief that the Baptist had made the burden of his preaching his annunciation of Jesus? At least a partial response is made in these verses.

"Are you he who is to come, or shall we look for another?" It is hard to miss a peremptory and challenging note in this question, which even contains an implied threat. "He who is to come" was virtually a technical term for the Messiah of Jewish expectation. That becomes precisely the point at issue, of course, and contributes a special poignancy to Jesus's reply, which at first glance seems to be no reply at all, simply telling John's disciples and John himself to look about themselves and verify what they already know. Jesus alludes to such signs of the messianic age as we saw detailed in our first reading from the book of Isaiah. The blind see, the lame walk, the lepers are cleansed, the deaf hear, the dead are raised, and the poor and oppressed have preached to them the good news of God's deliverance. These signs have been fulfilled in Jesus; but such was already known and was, in fact, the presupposed occasion of these disciples' query. For these signs are only preliminary to the ultimate certification of Jesus as "he who is to come."

The kingdom envisaged by John the Baptist which had been eagerly embraced by his disciples included as a prime component the apocalyptic messiah of Jewish nationalist hope, the avenger of ancient wrongs, the one who would humble Gentile oppressors like the Romans and their puppets, and free the enslaved and the imprisoned like John himself. The question posed by John through his disciples amounts, then, to a challenge and a call to action: If indeed you are the Messiah, then act like the Messiah and manifest your overwhelming power! This is the kind of messiahship to which Jesus was tempted, according to Matt. 4:1–11; Luke 4:1–13.

We have seen often in these readings the theme that God's fulfillment of his promises may come about in unexpected ways, not at all in any necessary accord with the conceptions of those who had waited on that fulfillment. And thus Jesus's real answer to the Baptist consists in his counterchallenge of faith: "Blessed is he who takes no offense at me." Not even the Baptist is exempt from the rule to which all are subject: the faith that saves and gives access to the kingdom of God comes through hearing and receiving God's Word as and when it is uttered, not necessarily through a satisfying confirmation of prior thoughts and intimations.

The commendation of the Baptist that follows is at the same time Jesus's way of defining the other's proper place in the divine plan of salvation. Jesus turns to "the crowds"—with whom Matthew would have his readers identify themselves, that they might here and now have corrected any misunderstandings they might entertain with regard to John the Baptist's role in relation to Jesus. What, he asks, was the popular estimation of the Baptist? What was the nature of this man to whom all of Judea had gone out into the desert to see and hear? This was a question that troubled many and was avoided by many (cf. Mark 11:30–32 and parallels). Was he really a reed shaken by the wind? Some had doubtless been put off by John's apparent powerlessness in confrontation with the palace politics surrounding Antipas. Others had been puzzled and beguiled by his unconventional way of life, a cause of scandal (Luke 7:33) or of invidious comparisons (Mark 2:18). Jesus dismisses these incidentals as of no consequence. If they were looking for a messenger of cheer and comfort, he says ironically, they should seek him in Antipas's palace rather than in his dungeon. But most of the people had thought him a prophet, and they had been right. They had even been right in thinking him more than a prophet. They had been right without knowing it, for though he was not the Messiah as many had believed, still he was the immediate prophet of the

Messiah, fulfilling the words of Mal. 3:1 concerning one who would be another Elijah. Yes, Jesus will affirm an even higher title for John: never has the earth known one greater than he. And yet, and yet . . . the least in the kingdom of heaven is greater than he.

This paradox is easily resolved. The measure of "greatness" in these comparisons is not personal character but providential function. John the Baptist is the last and the greatest of the figures of the Old Testament, the preparatory dispensation. Like Moses he stands on the threshold of the promised land but does not—neither as prophet nor one more than prophet—enter into it. John's personal relation to God is not a question that rises here. What we are being told is that in relation to God's economy of salvation he is defined solely in terms of his proximity to Jesus Christ.

We are also so defined. Jesus's words are no denigration of the Baptist, and we who count ourselves, or aspire to count ourselves, as belonging to the kingdom are not invited by his words to glory in some imagined superiority over John. We are invited, rather, to give glory to God who has bestowed on us through grace and no merit of our own a prize for which prophets and wise men had yearned for ages, and whose hopes have been rewarded only in our time, the time of the church.

The Fourth Sunday in Advent

Lutheran	Roman Catholic	Episcopal	Pres/UCC/Chr	Meth/COCU
Isa. 7:10–14 (15–17)	Isa. 7:10–14	Isa. 7:10–14	Isa. 7:10–15	Isa. 7:10–17
Rom. 1:1–7	Rom. 1:1–7	Rom. 1:1–7	Rom. 1:1–7	Rom. 1:1–7
Matt. 1:18–25	Matt. 1:18–24	Matt. 1:18–25	Matt. 1:18–25	Matt. 1:18–25

FIRST LESSON: ISAIAH 7:10–17

This well-known Isaian passage about the coming of Immanuel has been put in the context of the so-called Syro-Ephraimite war. It was on this occasion, according to the Bible, that King Pekah of Israel joined with Rezin of Syria in an effort to depose Ahaz of Judah and replace him with "the son of Tabeel," probably a Davidic pretender of sorts, the product of the marriage of a Judean king with a princess of Beth Tabeel, an Aramean state in the northern Transjordan (2 Kings 16:5–9; Isa. 7:1–6). The aim, of course, was to put a puppet king on the throne who would do the bidding of Rezin and Pekah. Assyrian records unearthed by archaeology have provided additional information that allows us to put this episode in a larger perspective.

Rezin, the last Aramean king of Damascus, had assembled a coalition of the little states of Syria-Palestine to resist the imperialist expansion of Tiglath-pileser III, king of Assyria. In Palestine he secured the cooperation of Philistia and of Pekah of Ephraim (all that was soon to be left of the northern kingdom of Israel after Tiglath-pileser's annexation of Gilead and Galilee); Pekah was fresh from the assassination of his pro-Assyrian predecessor. But Judah refused to join the coalition. Thus the Syro-Ephraimite invasion, which turned out to be more bluster than anything else, was a detail only of Rezin's politics, an attempt to force Judah to join the common front against Assyria.

The issue of this politics was disaster on all sides. Tiglath-pileser picked off his enemies one by one. Rezin was captured and executed. Pekah was assassinated at the instigation of the pro-Assyrian Hoshea, who replaced him as the last king of Israel. Ahaz of Judah was driven in self-defense into total reliance on Assyria, whose vassal he became and to whose ways he conformed himself to the ultimate extent of turning the temple of the Lord into a house of heathen worship and sacrificing his own son as a burnt offering in the forbidden rites of Canaan (2 Kings 16:1–4, 10–20). This last mentioned, the sacrifice of a son who was also presumably his firstborn and therefore heir to the throne, lends a special pathos to Isaiah's prophecy of the Immanuel.

The pathos is present, whatever the historical context of Isaiah's oracle. When v. 10 prefaces to our passage the note that it was "again" that the Lord spoke to Ahaz through Isaiah, we are left to wonder if it was on the same occasion as that of vv. 1–9, the Syro-Ephraimite invasion with its threat to the future of the Davidic kingship. In the mind of the editor of the Book of Isaiah the two passages were certainly connected, evidenced particularly in v. 9b, where the demand for faith on Ahaz's part implies that it is lacking. At all events, however, even if the reference to the "two kings" in v. 16 should be purely editorial, it is always the same Ahaz who is addressed, there is a danger confronting the royal succession, and it is to this problem that Isaiah speaks.

As was brought out in our observations on the Old Testament Lesson for the Second Sunday in Advent, Isaiah virtually alone of Israel's preexilic prophets shared the enthusiasm for the kingly ideal so often encountered in the "royal psalms" of the Psalter (Psalms 2, 45, 110, etc.). For Isaiah this ideal was bound up with the Davidic dynasty, based on the tradition of the covenant made with David by the God of Israel (Psalm 89; 2 Samuel 7). Drawing his inspiration from the cultural and religious heritage of Jerusalem, the city that David had made his own, Isaiah became in effect the originator of "prophetic messianism": belief not only in the perpetuity of the Davidic kingship but also in the coming of the king from that line who would be truly worthy to be called Son of God.

The terms of that covenant with David promised an everlasting dynasty even though unworthy kings would rise within it who would be individually punished. It is of this permanence that Isaiah seeks to reassure Ahaz in the passage before us, to which end he invites the king to ask of the Lord a sign, a sign of any magnitude, of any depth.

Ahaz hypocritically refuses to put the Lord to a test by asking for a sign. It is interesting to observe a coincidence of language here. The same verb is found in Gen. 22:1 of the Lord's putting Abraham to the test in respect to his son Isaac. Abraham proved his faith by his willingness to sacrifice his son. Ahaz, by sacrificing his son, whether or not this had already occurred at the time of this confrontation, abandoned his faith. There is irony, therefore, in Isaiah's challenging Ahaz to request a sign from "the Lord your God."

Since Ahaz will not ask for a sign, then he will be given one despite himself, a sign that will be vastly different from what he might have wished. The Lord has both good and ill in store for the king and his people. Even the good, however, Ahaz would hardly have recognized as such, for it is to be the continued presence of Yahweh, the God of Israel, among his people. Ahaz's apostasy will not prevail. There will be a worthier scion of the house of David to guarantee this. As for the evil, in spite of all of Ahaz's plotting and scheming and what he would have called political realism, disaster in its worst Assyrian form will surely descend upon Judah.

The sign given to Ahaz against his will is of a young woman—*the* young woman, actually—conceiving and bearing a son whose name shall be called Immanuel. It seems reasonable to accept a common understanding of these words, namely, that the prophet had in mind the coming king Hezekiah and his royal mother, presumably Abi the daughter of Zechariah (2 Kings 18:2). Hezekiah, whose reign was to draw almost unqualified praise from the Deuteronomic authors of the Book of Kings, did embody and realize in his life and career many of the ideals that were predicated of Davidic kingship.

But Hezekiah is, in the prophet's mind, part of a sign and not yet its full realization. Immanuel, "God with us," is a hope, like the name of Hezekiah itself, "Yahweh is my strength." He is a sign of salvation: when he comes to accountability ("when he knows how to refuse the evil and choose the good") he will be eating curds and honey. The meaning of this expression is debated, but it seems preferable to take it as a mark of prosperity and well-being. But he is also a sign of that disaster that is to come.

For Hezekiah is also remembered for his hopeless resistance to Assyria which ended in Sennacherib's invasion in 701 B.C. The Bible puts the best face possible on the invasion from Hezekiah's standpoint (2 Kings 18:13—19:37; Isaiah 36—37), while Sennacherib's annals do the same from his standpoint. Jerusalem, it is true, was spared, but Judah was laid waste. The hope expressed in Immanuel remained unfulfilled. For fulfillment we must look to the Gospel of today.

SECOND LESSON: ROMANS 1:1–7

Paul is introducing himself to the Roman church, a church which he himself had not founded and to whom he was known only by reputation. As is usual in his letters he follows the epistolary conventions of the time, which called for an identification of sender and recipient followed by a stylized greeting and the establishment of some common grounds of rapport before the statement of the actual business of the letter. Frequently he adapts these conventions to his own special purposes, as he does here in a quite masterful fashion.

First of all, he is Paul, but not immediately "the apostle," as in his other later letters. Rather, he is, like the Romans, a servant of Jesus Christ, but one called to be an apostle. This approach allows him to develop the idea of what it is to be an apostle and specifically what is the nature of his apostleship and how that should be of concern to the Romans. The last appears only toward the end of Paul's long sentence—for all of the seven verses make up a single sentence in Paul's original—when he specifies as his part in the gospel of God that of bringing the Gentiles to the obedience of faith. Thus Paul asserts his claim to a hearing from what must have been at least a predominately Gentile church at Rome.

But he has also done something that is even more significant. The RSV of vv. 3–4 has obscured, perhaps inevitably in translation, the use and adaptation that Paul seems to have made of an older credal formula—perhaps it was a formula of the Roman church, or at least one that was well known there—as part of his establishing rapport between himself and his readers. Quite literally rendered, it was confessed of Jesus that he was

> born—of the seed of David—according to the flesh;
> constituted—son of God—according to the spirit.

We think that this is not, or was not, Paul's own formula to begin with mainly because "flesh" and "spirit," certainly one of Paul's favorite dichotomies, do not have here the meaning he ordinarily gives them. Here they do not serve as synonyms for "darkness" and "light," as they normally would in the Pauline sense, but rather contrast the order of nature with the working out of God's salvific plan. In this plan, the order of the spirit, Jesus of Nazareth, a Jew of Davidic descent, has been constituted by God—the "designated" of RSV is perhaps too weak an expression—the instrument of his salvation, Savior, Son of God.

Son of God *in power,* the text now reads. These words may have been original to the formula but are probably a Pauline adaptation. In any case they help to clarify what is involved here: It is not Christ's connatural sonship with the Father that is a issue, but his character as the medium of God's redemptive power. Probably Paul, too, has added the qualification "of holiness" to characterize the Spirit. This is not simply a Semitism for "Holy Spirit." Holiness is for Paul an active concept: it is the Spirit that makes us holy. And almost certainly it is Paul on his own who has specified the "how" of Jesus Christ's having been constituted Son of God in power—namely by his having been raised from the dead. For Paul, the resurrection of Jesus was not merely the proclamation but also the very means of God's making him a Savior, one who is now "alive to God" with an eternal life which we may hope to share who are united with him by faith (Rom. 6:5–11).

So did Paul, an apostle of the gospel of God promised beforehand through his prophets, introduce himself to the Romans, sharing with them a common faith in a Son of God in power. It was the same salvific sonship with the divine that Isaiah had celebrated and ascribed to the scion of the house of David of his time, but now realized in ways that the prophet could scarcely have imagined. This reading from Romans facilitates the transition from Isaiah to Matthew, who also, but in his own way, finds in the coming of Jesus the fulfillment of ancient prophecy.

GOSPEL: MATTHEW 1:18–25

Matthew's parallel to the Annunciation scene with which Luke and Christian art have made us so familiar lies in these verses, though it is characteristic of Matthew that the announcement is made to Joseph rather than to Mary. The recipient of the annunciation, however, is not the main point at issue. Nor, for that matter, is the annunciation itself, except to the extent that it is integral to the assertion of the miracle that was the birth of Jesus Christ.

Matthew's qualification of Joseph as "a just man" probably means that he thought of him as exemplifying the kind of righteous conduct that Jesus came to inculcate, the spirit of "the law and the prophets" (Matt. 5:17). Faced with the uncomfortable fact of his betrothed's evident pregnancy, yet unwilling to make a public spectacle of her as the letter of the law might dictate, he had resolved upon the expedient of a quiet divorce. The ancient law that had decreed death by stoning for an errant bride, later mitigated by custom to death by strangulation, was now under Roman rule dead letter, but the shame and obloquy that would attach to the public repudiation of a prospective wife would have been scarcely preferable to death in the closed society of Jewish life.

It is only through the subsequent message of God that the perplexed Joseph is made aware of what Matthew has already told us, that Mary was with child of the Holy Spirit. As with the patriarchs of old, especially perhaps with Joseph's remote ancestor whose name he bore and whose descent into Egypt he was soon to emulate, this revelation of the divine purposes is made in a dream. "*That which* is conceived in her," he is told, is the result of the working of the Spirit of God. As in the Pauline passage above, this statement is concerned not with the divine nature of Christ, which was also an early Christian affirmation, but with his human nature that is soon to be made the instrument of

God's salvation. She, Mary, will bear a son who will save his people from their sins. Names are always pregnant with meaning in the Bible. Jesus, the Greek form of the Hebrew or Aramaic *Yeshua,* is also the Septuagint title of the book of Joshua: the two Semitic names are variants of each other. Some years ago an ossuary (a postinterment bone-box in which the remains of pious Jews were transported to Jerusalem) was discovered bearing the legend: "Jesus the son of Joseph." Probably no two names of males were more common in first-century Palestine than these. But *Yeshua* is also of the same root in Hebrew as the words "save" and "salvation." For Matthew, therefore, "Jesus" had much the same significance that "Immanuel" or "Hezekiah" had for Isaiah.

And now Matthew finds in the Immanuel prophecy a direct linkage with the "way" that Jesus' birth took place (v. 18). It was by virginal conception. In making this appropriation of prophetic words, a thing Matthew does much more often than the other evangelists, he was aided immeasurably by the translation the Septuagint Greek had made of the *'almah,* "young woman," of Isa. 7:14. In the Greek the rendering was *parthenos,* a word that almost invariably signified a virgin. It is in this Greek form that Matthew finds his prophecy of what we commonly call the virgin birth of Jesus.

We may wonder whether the Hellenist Jewish translator of the book of Isaiah had thought that the Messiah to come would be born of a virgin. Possibly he had, but probably he had not. Probably he intended by *parthenos* to do nothing more than offer an equivalent of *'almah,* a young woman of marriageable age. Jewish tradition and legend—though we cannot always be sure of what went on in the speculations of the Hellenistic Jewish Diaspora—knew nothing of virgin births, however much embroidered the tales of marvelous portents and cosmic disturbances that had accompanied the appearance in the world of Abraham, Moses, and others, may be.

Whatever is to be made of the tradition of Jesus' virginal conception—that it is a relatively late tradition, that it seems to have been unknown to Mark, John, or Paul, that it is a mythical portrayal of Jesus' unique relation to God, and so on—it is in any construction a Christian tradition. There is nothing, as far as we know, from which it could have been copied in the traditions of Judaism. Also, again as far as we know, there is no real parallel to it in the legends and mythologies of the Gentiles. When the author of the First Gospel concludes his little account of the "way" of Jesus' birth, therefore, he voices a belief that had developed exclusively in Christian circles. Joseph took his wife: fortified by what God had made known to him, he did not hesitate to receive Mary his betrothed into his house and conclude the legalities of marriage. But he "knew" her not in the way of husband and wife before she had borne her son Jesus.

The Nativity of Our Lord, Christmas Day

Lutheran	Roman Catholic	Episcopal	Pres/UCC/Chr	Meth/COCU
Isa. 9:2–7	Isa. 9:2–7	Isa. 9:2–4, 6–7	Isa. 9:2, 6–7	Isa. 9:1–7
Titus 2:11–14	Titus 2:11–14	Titus 2:11–14	Titus 2:11–15	Titus 2:11–15
Luke 2:1–20	Luke 2:1–14	Luke 2:1–14 (15–20)	Luke 2:1–14	Luke 2:1–20

FIRST LESSON: ISAIAH 9:2–7

Isaiah 9:2–7 (in RSV; 9:1–6 in the Hebrew text and other English versions) has been put in the context of a prophecy of salvation for those Israelites who had once inhabited the north of Israel that had now become "Galilee of the nations." These were the Israelites who had been engulfed by the Assyrian conquests of 733–732 B.C., who had been scattered abroad into various parts of the Assyrian empire as victims of the imperial policy of divide and rule, and whose place had been taken over largely by other, foreign elements imported from other parts of the empire. This context is secondary to the content of the prophecy. It is conceivably original with Isaiah, but much more likely it is postexilic, part of a nationalist enthusiasm which looked forward to a restoration of the traditional Israel of the past, north and south, in a new polity that would be provided by the Lord. This was a restoration that was never to be, not at least as it was then imaged.

Apart from the alleged historical context, the prophecy stands on its own, in sequence with that of Isaiah 7 which we read last Sunday. It is, in fact, its complement, another prophecy of that reign of everlasting justice and righteousness of which the birth of Immanuel was a hopeful sign. In this passage the "birth" of the king—again, in all probability, Hezekiah—upon which is based a renewed hope for a kingly reign that may rightly be acknowledged as that of God's anointed, is not his physical beginning but his beginning as king: his enthronement or near enthronement. "A child is born, a son is given" were appropriate acclamations when the royal scion ceased being the heir apparent and was actually enthroned as king: then he was constituted God's son and God became his father (2 Sam. 7:14; Ps. 2:7). The government—the scepter of royal authority—then descended upon his shoulder and remained, and he acquired the marvelous titles bestowed on him in v. 6.

These titles beautifully spell out the function of the Davidic king in the economy of God's providence. They simultaneously celebrate the royal dignity and stress its limitations, even as the conclusion of the oracle in v. 7 reminds us that it is not the king so much as the Lord of hosts who will effect what is promised. "Zeal," incidentally, is a relatively mild word to use in this connection. The Hebrew term denotes a fierce protective love for one's own. The Near Eastern royal mystique which encouraged great expectations regarding the king was shared by Israel, but shared in Israel's own way. The king, yes, but the king only as he embodied God's spirit and power. Hence the titles.

"Counselor," "Mighty One" *(gibbor)*, "Father," "Prince"—all these are names that may be borne by a king. But it is probably significant that the word "king" itself is avoided, even though it is very clear that a king was meant, and a Davidic king at that. It is as though the prophet wanted to demythify that royal mystique in this way as he certainly did in others. For that is the function of the qualifications that modify the kingly titles. The Counselor is Wonderful: the word *pele* that occurs here is usually a collective noun, referring to those miraculous deeds that surpass human powers, which only God can perform (Exod. 15:11; Isa. 25:1; Ps. 77:14 and countless other times in the Psalms). The *gibbor* will be *El gibbor,* Mighty God. Only in Ps. 45:6—and even there it can be debated—is an Israelite king called "god" flat out, though such usage was commonplace elsewhere in the Near East. Here the context is all: the king is not God but God's surrogate. So *Everlasting* Father: another attribute that belongs properly to God alone, through whose power alone the kingdom will be established for evermore. And finally, Prince of Peace. Peace *(shalom),* it is true, is too pervasive a concept in the Old Testament to be reserved to God alone. But again, in context, what is meant is that peace which God gives his people (Ps. 29:11).

Because of this faith, not in man but in what God can make man do, the liberation of vv. 2–5 is confidently foretold: the breaking of all the bonds that can be forged by man independently of and in opposition to God. "The day of Midian" must have meant to an Israelite audience some almost indescribably exhilarating triumph. Maybe it was the recollection of Gideon's victory recounted in Judg. 7:15–25. Maybe it was some other great event of which we have no further information.

This reading, as we have tried to explain it, should be seen as having a peculiar relevance to Christmas. The words of the prophet found in the coming of Jesus an incarnation that would turn his metaphors into realities whose magnitude he would not possibly have anticipated in the conditions of his time and place. But they were also realities which, even at Jesus's birth, remained hidden till the purposes of God in them were finally revealed. At Christmas we celebrate in a special way the humanity of our Lord, his becoming one with us. It is right that we should experience the joy of this event and want to share it with one another, joy of our common humanity rendered uncommon by his taking it upon himself. But this should also be the occasion to remind ourselves that the true glorification of our humanity came about not in the potential of Christmas, the first stage, but in the consummation of Easter, the last stage, when Jesus was constituted Son of God in power to be our Savior.

SECOND LESSON: TITUS 2:11–14

This little reading from one of the neglected Pastoral Epistles is a deceptively simple exhortation to a sober and upright life while we wait for the glorious appearance—the author uses the word "epiphany"—of God and Christ. It, too, the more we reflect on it, is singularly appropriate for a Christmas reading. This is so because it so clearly sums up the enduring effect of Christ's having come into the world in the first place, so that as a result those who have become united with him now live in two worlds, both awaiting a salvation that pertains only to the world (literally, "the age") that is to come, and at the same time rejoicing in that selfsame salvation that is already at work in this age.

That paradox of Christian living in this world is brought out in the language used to describe this work of God: while we await in hope the *epiphaneia* of the coming age, we are sustained by the grace of this salvation for all people which has already appeared, *epephane,* among us. That grace of salvation in which we rejoice, moreover, is not merely a historical event. It is an abiding presence that teaches us to live here and now the life of the world to come to which we truly belong. The faith in Christ upon which our hope rests—faith in him who gave himself for us to redeem us—cannot be, if it is true faith, a mere acquiescence to a gift of God. This grace is not one that can be passively accepted. For its working in us is to produce a people zealous for good deeds, for the godly life in this world that anticipates that of the next world.

The year-by-year experience of Christmas which never fails to gladden the Christian heart should also tell us that this godly life to which we are called in this world should be no life of gloom but rather presage the joy of the life of the world to come. Proverbially Christmas is a season of good feelings, of openness to others in a common rejoicing in the human spirit, of the performance of those "good deeds" of which our text speaks, by all who are touched by it however transitorily. It is an experience to which nonbelievers are hardly immune, as is witnessed by the Christmas celebrations of a secular society such as our own. We really should not affect to despise the secularized Christmas as unworthy of our recognition. Sentimentality and extravagances aside, it can also be a confirmation of the early church fathers' confidence in *anima humana naturaliter christiana:* that the instincts of our common humanity are in natural accord with the Christian experience. As Christians we recognize that Christmas joy is meaningless if it ends in good feelings only, and sometimes, to our discomfort, it is practitioners of the secular Christmas who teach us what, positively, it is "to renounce irreligion and worldly passions."

The RSV margin tells us that in v. 13 an alternative translation of the formula "our great God and Savior Jesus Christ" is "the great God and our Savior Jesus Christ"—that is, that the reference is to two persons and not one. The alternative is probably to be preferred. "The Great God" was a consecrated Jewish term for the one whom Jesus called his Father, and though the New Testament does not on occasion hesitate to affirm the divinity of Christ, it is doubtful that this precise title would have been applied to him. "God" and "Savior" are intimately joined in this verse, governed by a single Greek article. But that is also the case with the customary Pauline greeting "grace and peace from God-our-Father-and-Lord-Jesus Christ," where the persons are clearly distinguished while at the same time they are said to work as one. Thus understood, our text is christologically more meaningful, not less. We await the epiphany of a Savior who is the executor of a saving God.

GOSPEL: LUKE 2:1–20

This is, of course, the almost inevitable Gospel reading for Christmas Day. Its cadences are so familiar to us from our reading and hearing it over the years that there would seem to be little that might be deemed appropriate by way of commentary. Certainly this is not the place to discuss the issues of history or of historical verisimilitude raised by the piece: what is to be said, for example, of a census carried out in Palestine by Quirinius (Cyrinus) the governor of the Roman province of Syria, or of the alleged practice of enrolling heads of households in their ancestral towns and cities, or of the season of the year at which time shepherds would have been likely to tend their flocks in the open air, and so on. Nor does it seem to be indicated that we initiate a comparison of the Lukan and the Matthean birth and infancy stories, to ask to what degree they can be harmonized, for example. The Christmas story as it has developed in Christian piety and become crystallized in our devotional creches and classical art renders such excursions, for our purposes, rather otiose if not an actual obstacle to the appreciation of Christmas as a religious festival.

What we can do, perhaps, is take the story in the spirit in which it was written, at its face value, and try to make it the focus of our bringing together the message of other readings we have encountered in the course of this Advent and Christmas season.

As Luke tells the story, it is an exemplification of one of his primary convictions, that God has highly favored the lowly and the least likely; this theme he already anticipated in his portrait of Mary of Nazareth, the humble handmaiden of the Lord chosen to be the mother of the Messiah (Luke 1:26–56). Isaiah 9, our first reading, was at pains to point out that the most exalted of messianic titles signified nothing if not the powerlessness of even royal might alone to effect the kingdom of God: royal might apart from the zeal of the Lord of hosts is a vain display.

And so, our story. Jesus journeys a prisoner in his mother's womb from the mean town of Nazareth to the royal city of David, but hardly as a king. He comes to receive no royal plaudits but only because of the constraint of a law not of his making, a law which in his helplessness he could neither choose to obey nor to disregard. And once in Bethlehem, for him and his parents there is no place in the inn. This famous phrase means precisely what it says, without romanticism or rhapsodizing. These were common folk, strangers, without privilege, without "connections." They had to take their chances, to stand in line, to expect to fare no better and no worse than the rest of their fellow Jews thronging the city. And so Jesus is born under the humblest of circumstances imaginable, in a stable for cattle, his first resting place on earth a feeding trough. Even the swaddling cloths in which he is wrapped by his mother contribute to the theme. These were the simple means dictated by folk wisdom to safeguard the fragile body of a new baby so that it would develop straight and strong. The swaddling cloths, too, are part of that utter human ordinariness in which God has chosen to conceal his works of wonder. They are part of the "sign" given to the shepherds of the birth of a Savior who is Christ the Lord.

And the shepherds. Here are no magi from the East come to bow down and worship him who is born king of the Jews. The annunciation of this birth is made to simple, fearful men to whom is given for sign a scene that each had probably witnessed hundreds of times before: a newborn baby wrapped in swaddling cloths—a sign for faith, surely, like the sign of Immanuel offered to Ahaz, but otherwise devoid of significance. The song of the heavenly host underscores the message: divine peace, salvation, is being proclaimed to all who are of God's good will, to those whom he has chosen. This "thing" (literally, "this word") which the shepherds must see in Bethlehem, for which they glorify God and of which they become the first evangelists, can be seen only by faith just as it has been heard only by faith.

We are left to imagine what success, if any, greeted the testimony of these early believers. All who heard them wondered, we are told. To wonder is not necessarily to believe (cf. Luke 2:47; 24:22), though it may precede belief. It is possible that the shepherds' story was taken to be an idle tale, like the report of the women who were the first witnesses to the resurrection of Jesus (Luke 24:11). In contrast with this wonderment—wondering in the Orient is rarely silent—Mary is said to have pondered these things in her heart. This expression is almost identical with the Greek text in Dan. 7:28. (There are frequent allusions to the book of Daniel in Luke's narrative of Jesus' nativity and childhood.) The expression means that she kept these things to herself, for more mature reflection on their purport. Something similar is said of Mary in 1:29 and 2:51. As we shall have occasion to note later on, in this Gospel the mother of Jesus sometimes has an ecclesiological significance, as an ideal believer who seeks to penetrate the mysteries of God.

Luke's Christmas story is above all a story of the humanity of Christ, as Christian piety has always rightly perceived it. It is, in addition, a story that glories in the weakness and inadequacies of this humanity, that it may the better show forth the glory of God who has touched it and entered it. For "God chose what is low and despised in the world, even things that are not, to bring to nothing things that are" (1 Cor. 1:28).

The First Sunday After Christmas

Lutheran	Roman Catholic	Episcopal	Pres/UCC/Chr	Meth/COCU
Isa. 63:7–9	Sir. 3:2–6, 12–14	Isa. 61:10—62:3	Eccles. 3:1–9, 14–17	Isa. 63:7–9 or Eccles. 3:1–9, 14–17 or Sir. 3:2–6, 12–14
Gal. 4:4–7	Col. 3:12–21	Gal. 3:23–25; 4:4–7	Col. 3:12–17	Gal. 4:4–7
Matt. 2:13–15, 19–23	Matt. 2:13–15, 19–23	John 1:1–18	Matt. 2:13–15, 19–23	John 1:1–18

FIRST LESSON: ISAIAH 63:7–9

When we read this passage, which by all accounts is one of the most beautiful poems in the Old Testament, it is perhaps just as well that we pass over its immediate context, which is vv. 1–6. There a divine warrior—it seems to be the Lord himself—is pictured coming up from the land of Edom with his garments soaked with the blood of Israel's enemies who have been crushed and trampled into the ground in the way grapes are crushed and pulped in a winepress. It is pointless to try to mitigate the fierce hatred that obviously permeates this dramatic interlude, and it is equally pointless to try to explain it away. (Some of the early Christian writers wanted to reinterpret the whole thing as a portrayal of Christ fresh from the crucifixion, stained with the blood of his sacrifice.) The sentiments cannot be justified, they can only be explained. The verses evidently derive from a time when the memory was still very fresh of the perfidy of Edom, a jackal to the Babylonian lion, which did not hesitate to pick the bones of its prostrate neighbor after the Chaldeans had laid Jerusalem waste and destroyed its temple (cf. Psalm 137). The poet's humor is grim: right it was that Edom, the ''red land,'' should be red indeed, running with its own blood.

It is typical of the Old Testament that we should find the delightful poem of today's reading embedded in a scenario of revenge that we do not want to share, or at least we hope that we do not want to share. Our poem is part of a prayer to God that he will restore his people in this their time of degradation and ignominy, not, however, simply for their own well-being but that the Lord himself be recognized as a God who makes good on his own promises and is true to himself: that his name be known to his adversaries and that the nations may tremble in his presence (cf. 64:2). As is customary in these cries of distress and pleas for redress, whether of an individual client of the Lord or of the whole supplicant nation, ''motivation'' is offered the Lord in the form of a reminder of his past deeds of mercy and fidelity. That motivation we have here in vv. 7–9.

The psalmist recounts the steadfast love of the Lord, which forms the burden of his hymn of praise. ''Steadfast love'' involves the concept of *ḥesed,* that Hebrew word which has always defied an adequate translation. It means, whether on the part of God or of a human person, that love which rises from commitment to a relationship, one that is either natural—familial piety of father to son, child to parent, kinsman to kinsman, and the like—or one that has been formed by the plighted word—husband to wife, friend to friend, partner to partner, superior to subject, master to servant, or servant to master. In this context it is the *ḥesed* of the covenant that is in question: the loving concern for his people to which the Lord freely bound himself in choosing them to be his own in a very special way. It is also significant that here the word *ḥesed* appears in the plural: this steadfast love is not abstract virtue but a love that has been made manifest in concrete acts, a love that has proved itself and thereby has become real

This steadfast love, the psalmist affirms, the Lord has granted to Israel as a free gift. Why? Because it was in accord with his mercy. Mercy, *raḥamim,* involves another word and concept that is frequent in covenant language, but which also transcends it. It is a word related to *reḥem,* "womb," and therefore has some obvious connections with the tender, spontaneous, instinctive love and concern that a mother has for the offspring of her body, or, as in this case, a creator for the creatures that he has called into being. It is a love that is summoned forth by no commitment other than that which comes naturally, the disposition of the benign and openhearted that prompts them to protect and show mercy to the weak and defenseless. In the Bible *raḥamim* always implies the condescension of one above to one below.

It is this quality of the Lord's unstrained mercy that answered for the Israelites a question that occurred to them long before it did to others: Why did the Lord choose us to be his special people, to suffer affliction when we are afflicted, to redeem us, to carry us about in his arms? (The "redeem" of v. 9, it must be pointed out, has nothing to do with the commercial transaction that is implied by our conventional translations. The word refers, rather, to the obligations of family duty, to vindicate one's own physically or spiritually.) When Israel asked itself this question, it could only reply: "It was not because you were more in number than any other people that the Lord set his love upon you and chose you, for you were the fewest of all peoples; but it is because the Lord loves you" (Deut. 7:7–8).

We are invited in this post-Christmas time to thank God for the acts of his steadfast love and mercy which have eclipsed but not denigrated the salvation he repeatedly bestowed on the children of Israel, our fathers and mothers in the faith. We should not ignore the condition of God's salvation, however, which is accorded to those "who will not deal falsely" with the Lord. Covenant, though not a contract of our devising but rather a favor offered us, at all events demands of us conduct worthy of the Lord's chosen.

One final remark. The troublesome and puzzling "angel of his presence'' of RSV v. 9 is best got rid of as a makeshift translation trying to make sense of a Hebrew text that has become permanently damaged. Various modern English versions of the Bible (e.g., NEB, NAB) have judged that the Septuagint Greek Old Testament has preserved more accurately what the author originally said, which was: "It was no angel, no envoy, but he himself that delivered them."

SECOND LESSON: GALATIANS 4:4–7

In this passage Paul, too, is celebrating an act of God's fidelity to his promises, an exercise of the *hesed* of the Isaian text. It is, of course, a fulfillment far less provisional than the ones previously spoken of. "When the time had fully come." This is the time whose fullness is calculated by God, not by man.

Paul's context places these verses in an argument of deep consequence. He was trying to persuade the Galatians, as we know, that the redemption achieved in Christ Jesus had rendered the practice of the Mosaic law at best otiose, at worst a denial of Christ. Of course it could continue to be observed by Jewish Christians not for the sake of righteousness but simply as a part of cultural tradition, as in fact Paul observed it himself. But the Galatians were not Jews, and the law was not of their culture. For them to submit themselves, as they had been told they should, to observances that pertained to the time of the world-without-Christ, when the world was still subject to "the elemental spirits of the universe" (v. 3), meant that they were abandoning the gospel, as indeed Paul accuses them of doing in Gal. 1:6. His argument is that the law served only a temporary purpose in God's economy, that that purpose had now been accomplished, and that the greater salvific design of God in which the law was but an interlude had now been played out in the redemption accomplished in and through Christ.

In these verses he introduces another consideration. In any economy (remember, the word means "housekeeping") it is slaves and servants who are subject to rules and regulations, and among these, for the time being at least, must also be counted minor children who are at the beck and call of guardians and trustees; but the heir of the household, when he attains his majority, is free of all this, master of his own estate. Now, says Paul, in Christ all of us, Jew and Gentile, have been constituted heirs of the promise, in fact and not in expectation. Q.E.D., then, as regards the law.

Paul first deals with the liberation of the Jews. When *we* were children, *we* were slaves to the elements of the world, to which the law pertained. But God sent his Son, born of woman, born under the law, to redeem those who were under the law. It was observed centuries ago by St. Thomas Aquinas in his commentary on Galatians how essential to Paul's argument is the fact of the humanity, indeed the very Jewishness, of Jesus of Nazareth—a stress that is hardly characteristic of Paul. Hence Aquinas insisted at some length that the text spoke of Jesus as "made" rather than merely "born." (The Greek verb translated "born" by RSV does, in fact, often mean "made" or "created," depending on the context. Aquinas, of course, was dependent on the Latin translation of the text.) In union with Christ, God's Son, all those subject to the law as he became subject to it have with him fulfilled the law and become free of it, and, still in union with him, have been adopted as God's sons and heirs.

But not only the Jews, also *you* the Gentiles have become sons and heirs in Christ. Elsewhere but not here Paul explains the rationale whereby the Gentiles share in the promise first given to Israel: through a common faith with Abraham, the father of the faithful who preceded the law. Here Paul appeals to the Galatians to accept the testimony of their own experience to the fact that they are heirs and not slaves. "God has sent the Spirit of this Son into our hearts, crying, 'Abba! Father!'" The familiar language in which Jesus addressed his Father the Galatians do not hesitate to make their own. They profess themselves, therefore, to enjoy this familiarity with God.

In calling to mind the familiar "Abba" of Jesus' address Paul is probably alluding to early Christian liturgical usage of this Aramaic word. But it is evident also that he has in mind a reality that the liturgy can only emblematize. How and under what sign the Holy Spirit makes his presence known to provide that confidence and boldness by which the intimacy of Jesus with his Father is asserted to be shared by Christians are questions to be answered not only by the Galatians but by us as well. A chief evidence, no doubt, is the presence of fraternal charity: "By this sign . . . if you have love for one another." Children of a common father are also brothers and sisters of one another, bound together in a single family relationship. And of course, it is not just a local community of believers, nor yet a universal church, who make up the family of God, for every human being is potentially his child and heir.

GOSPEL: MATTHEW 2:13–15, 19–23

This Gospel reading, concluding Matthew's version of the events of Jesus's nativity and infancy with its accumulation of Old Testament testimonial texts, covers the two episodes of the flight of the Holy Family into Egypt and their settling down in Nazareth of Galilee, omitting the story of the slaying of the infants of Bethlehem by the order of Herod.

Of at least equal importance with Matthew's explicit citations of Old Testament prophecy in connection with the Lord's coming are the details of his story which by implication involve the history of the people of the Old Testament and particularly of Moses. We have remarked before on Matthew's studied effort to portray Jesus as a new Moses and a greater-than-Moses by any number of allusions and literary devices. Here we have this theme brought out in numerous ways: the Egyptian setting, a wicked king seeking the life of a child (cf. Exod. 1:22), the parallel of Matt. 2:20 with Exod. 4:19, and so forth. But of course the correspondences are not perfect, and the more than subtle differences between the two stories both outweigh them and put them in perspective.

For the wicked king this time is not Egyptian but Jewish—to the extent that the Jews most reluctantly had to count the Idumean Herod as one of their number (descendant of the hated Edomites of Isaiah 63). Egypt is no longer the place of oppression that it was for the Israelites of the exodus, but rather one of refuge and salvation, as in fact it has become, off and on, even in Old Testament times (1 Kings 11:40, for example). In Jesus' time Egypt was a province of the Roman Empire, and for the church of Matthew's Gospel Rome was still regarded as a benign influence in the world, a mainstay of order and law, a defense against the capricious power of barbarous kingdoms and ungoverned mobs. It was already recognized that the future of Christianity would lie not in Judea, the land of the Jews, but in the great Gentile world, symbolized for Matthew by Egypt and, possibly, Galilee ("Galilee of the nations," Isa. 9:1).

Warned, as usually, in a dream, Joseph takes Mary and the child Jesus into Egypt, where they remain until the death of Herod. The prophetic text that Matthew sees fulfilled thereby is that of Hos. 11:1: "Out of Egypt I called my son." In Hosea the reference is to the exodus, the first of the Lord's great works of salvation by which he freed the people of Israel from the bondage of Egypt. It is noteworthy that in this instance Matthew had to abandon the Septuagint version of the Old Testament in favor of a more literal Greek rendering of the text. For the Septuagint had translated the verse: "Out of Egypt I called his [Israel's] children."

After Herod's death Joseph is once more told in a dream to return to the land of Israel. But this time he is permitted by the divine messenger to exercise his own initiative to a point. On his own he learns that in Herod's stead now reigns one of his elder sons, Archelaus. Herod died in 4 B.C., according to our somewhat defective chronology, and the Romans appointed Archelaus to succeed him in Judea along with Samaria and Idumea, without, however, bestowing on him the prestigious title of "king": he remained forever a "tetrarch." Joseph, rightly assuming that he was the fruit of an evil tree, no better than Herod, therefore on his own initiative decided to settle in the village of Nazareth in Galilee. His forebodings about Archelaus were borne out in the event, for this despot soon became too much even for the Romans to stomach, and in A.D. 6 they deposed him. Thereafter Judea and Samaria came under direct Roman rule, as was the situation during the ministry of Jesus. Galilee was also a tetrarchy, ruled along with Perea by yet another of Herod's sons, Antipas, whom Herod had actually intended to be his sole heir. Obviously he was deemed preferable to his brother Archelaus, and, as a matter of fact, Antipas was the most capable and evenhanded of Herod's sons; he generally governed wisely, and his reluctant acquiescence to the execution of John the Baptist is not typical of his reign.

Matthew identifies as for the first time "a city called Nazareth," since unlike Luke he had no story that presumed Joseph and Mary to be native Galileans and residents of Nazareth to begin with. Far more importantly, he has found in the settling of the Holy Family there one more prophetic fulfillment: that he, Jesus, shall be called a Nazarene.

These words have provoked endless discussion and countless attempts at elucidation. We are not likely to shed additional light on the subject here, but we shall try. The reference is vague: "that what was spoken by the prophets might be fulfilled." By which prophets? Matthew's word translated "Nazarene" is actually *nazoraios*. Another word used in the New Testament (but not by Matthew), *nazarenos*, looks like a plausible adjective for Nazareth, as *nazoraios* does not. Judging from other words like *pharisaios*, Pharisee, and *saddoukaios,* Sadducee, *nazoraios* ought to come out in English something like Nazoree—but if it did, we would hardly know what to do with the word. In Talmudic and later Jewish writings Jesus is referred to as the *noṣri* and Christians as *noṣrim.* We do not know the origin of these terms or whether they have any connection with the New Testament *nazoraios.* But it is conceivable that these were pejorative words of some kind, and it does appear that Matthew thought of *nazoraios,* which he did associate with Nazareth, as a pejorative word. But what of the prophets?

Isaiah 11:1, in a passage we have seen in our readings for this season, used the word *neṣer* for the "branch" that would grow out of the roots of Jesse. Samson, in Judg. 16:17, at least in most of the textual transmission of the Septuagint, is given the title *naziraios,* transliterating the Hebrew *nazir.* The book of Judges in the later Jewish canon is listed among the "early prophets"; but would Samson have been considered a type of Christ? Needless to say, neither of these proposals offered as the background of Matthew's *nazoraios* has been greeted with much enthusiasm, and the same is true of the various other proposals. Some observers have simply concluded that Matthew, or the redactor of Matthew's Gospel, meant only to say that *any* event in the life of Jesus and *anything* that was said of him *must* on general principles have been foretold by the prophets.

At all events, Matthew probably intends to insinuate that in his lifetime Jesus endured, in Jewish eyes, the obloquy of a Galilean background—Galileans were classed by the Judeans as superiors only to the Samaritans, and "no prophet is to rise from Galilee" (John 7:52)—especially from a background centered at Nazareth, thought to be the last place on earth from which anything good was to be expected (John 1:46). The obloquy that God's emissaries are to expect is certainly a well-worn prophetic theme.

And that seems to be the principal idea we should take away from this ending of Matthew's story. It fits into the pattern of other readings of the season. Those who are accounted least in human terms may be accounted most by God. This fact is for all of us a hope and a consolation.

The Name of Jesus (January 1)

Lutheran	Roman Catholic	Episcopal	Pres/UCC/Chr
Num. 6:22–27	Num. 6:22–27	Exod. 34:1–8	Deut. 8:1–10
Rom. 1:1–7 or Phil. 2:9–13	Gal. 4:4–7	Rom. 1:1–7 or Phil. 2:9–13	Rev. 21:1–7
Luke 2:21	Luke 2:16–21	Luke 2:15–21	Matt. 25:31–46

FIRST LESSON: NUMBERS 6:22–27

The three readings of today fit together very nicely, as we shall soon see. The first of them is the Aaronic priestly blessing, a passage which in view of the evident influence it has exercised on Psalm 67 may be very old indeed among the documents the Old Testament has preserved. The context in which it is now found in the Book of Numbers—the postexilic legislation concerning the Nazirite vow—is nothing with which we need to bother. Blessings of this kind, which express some of the most elevated language ever used of God in any religious literature, are timeless and need no justification beyond the fact that they exist.

This is called a priestly blessing because, quite apart from its association with Aaron and his sons in its present context, blessings of this solemn kind were regarded as being the particular prerogative of the priesthood (Deut. 21:5). It was, in fact, probably a blessing pronounced by the Levitical priests in the Jerusalem temple before the exile. Jewish tradition holds that it accompanied the daily morning sacrifices in the temple and that when it was recited the sacred name of Yahweh was pronounced, not the usual substitute Adonai (our "Lord"). Later it was adopted in the synagogue service.

Though this does not show up in modern English translation where "you" can be either singular or plural, it is worthy of note that the recipient of the blessing is addressed throughout in the second person singular: "May Yahweh bless thee." We must not conclude from this fact that the blessing was originally intended for individual Israelites, like the expression of good wishes from one person to another. Addressing the whole people as a single "thou" is a characteristic of the parenetic or preaching style of Deuteronomy and the prophets, emphasizing their oneness both in weal and in woe. This familiar language, however, is an encouragement to all who are conscious of their status as members of a priestly people to have no hesitation about making the words of this blessing their own.

May the Lord bless you and keep you: the blessing regards both the positive and the negative. Deuteronomy 28:2–14 details what the blessing of the Lord would have meant to all of Israel. Blessing in the city and in the field, good crops, increase of cattle and the good things of life. And protection against enemies, the Lord watching over and guarding them in their blessed state. These are material goods, certainly, some of that healthy "materialism" of the Old Testament that we discussed in the reading of Isa. 35:1–10 for the Third Sunday of Advent. But they are goods prized specifically because they are the gifts and blessings of Israel's God in fidelity to his covenant promises, the exercise of his *ḥesed,* his steadfast love which expects a reciprocal *ḥesed* from his people.

May the Lord make his face to shine upon you. We would say, using no less a metaphor, may he smile upon you. The second part of this invocation explains and gives meaning to the first: may he be gracious to you. This last means precisely what it says. To "be gracious" does not denote simply good feelings, expansiveness, courtliness, amiability, all the qualifications that we attach to a comfortable benignity. It means, quite literally, the granting of grace, favor to the undeserving, or at least to those who have no claim upon it. The Old Testament was as conscious as we of the New Testament that the mercies of the Lord, which he bestows on whom he wills, cannot of their very nature be counted on except in hope, in reliance of the goodness, the *raḥamim,* the mercy, that comes naturally to him.

And finally, may he lift up his countenance upon you. This idiom, literally "to raise the face," frequent in the Old Testament, doubtless stems from court usage, signifying the nod of approval given to a petitioner, just as the companion expression, "To raise the head [of someone]," implies the lifting up of the head of a supplicant that has been bowed in humble submission (cf. Gen. 40:13). The explanatory complement is: may he give you peace. This is an additional example to those we have seen before where *shalom,* the condition of healing and wholeness, is presented as the salvific gift of God.

It remains to point out the special pertinence of this text to our other readings and to the holy Name of Jesus which we celebrate today. The threefold "Lord" of our vernacular versions of the Old Testament is, as we have already noted, the solemn threefold "Yahweh" of the Hebrew text. It is most fitting—indeed, the contrary would be singularly inappropriate in a translation of the Bible intended for Christian liturgical use—that we adopt this ancient surrogate in place of the "sectarian," or at least particularist proper name, under which Israel first knew its God. But of course the surrogate is not a Christian invention. It stands on an earlier Jewish convention which held the proper name of God in such awe that it was rarely pronounced—even to the extent that the correct pronunciation was forgotten, so that we cannot be absolutely sure of it today. The convention decreed that "Lord," in Aramaic or Greek, be the spoken word whatever might be the written word encountered in reading. The providential choice of this title of universal application should be borne in mind as we take up our next reading.

SECOND LESSON: PHILIPPIANS 2:9–3

We turn to the great christological hymn of Philippians, of which we have the final part along with the reason that the hymn has been included in the epistle. It is an arresting thought that this hymn, which by universal consent is a precious piece of early Christian confessional literature that conceivably even goes back to the church's Semitic origins, has been adopted and adapted by the Pauline author of Philippians simply as a motivation to the exercise of religious obedience. It is testimony, perhaps, to the high value he attached to obedience, but also, perhaps, to his relaxed and matter-of-fact acceptance of a theology that has provoked thousands of volumes of commentary through the centuries. And yet this attitude is not untypical of the New Testament, which so often seems far more interested in dwelling on the practical consequences of faith rather than on credal statements as such.

The hymn is pre-Pauline without being un-Pauline. That is to say, both in its use of an extraordinary number of words and concepts that are otherwise not to be found in the Pauline literature and in the relative primitiveness of some of its formulations it gives evidence of belonging to a stage of theological development that long preceded both the Pauline and the Johannine theologies which are the bedrock of New Testament christology. But at the same time, its presence in

Philippians with only the barest of editing and nuancing shows clearly enough that Paul, though he might have preferred to express his thoughts somewhat differently, would have found the theology of the hymn basically compatible with his own.

In context (v. 5), the example of Christ is proposed not precisely as a model to be imitated—since Christ is unique, this would be an impossibility—but as having by a self-immolation proper to himself made possible that "mind," that climate of faith, in which the believer is encouraged to set aside egotism and to allow the working out of salvation "in fear and trembling." Obedience is more than respect for apostolic leadership or the good order of authority willed by God, though it does in fact include all of this. Obedience is also realistic self-appraisal, the humility to recognize one's limitations and the inability to "make it on one's own," and above all to acknowledge the realities of cause and effect, of life as it is, and of things as they are. It is to acquiesce humbly in the knowledge that only because God is in us both to will and to achieve that salvation is within our grasp.

The "therefore" of v. 9 relates Christ's exaltation—the word is actually "superexaltation"—to his prior "emptying" and "humbling" of himself and his "becoming obedient" even unto death that are described in vv. 6–8. In what did this humiliation consist? Not in the incarnation alone: nowhere in the New Testament is the incarnation characterized as a humiliation; it is, rather, an act of divine condescension declaring that human nature, first called forth to be the image and likeness of God, worthy and fit to coexist with God in his fullness. But the incarnation is part of the obedience of Christ which led to his final humiliation. By this obedience Christ divested himself of the divine condition that was by nature his and abandoned himself to the will of God even to death. "Even to death" of itself is nothing more or less than the natural terminus of what it is to be "in the likeness of men" or "in human form": it is as natural for human beings to die as it is to be born. But we may suspect the presence of a Pauline clarification in the added words: "even death on a cross." These words take us from the realm of the speculative and plant us on the firm historical ground of Jesus the Christ. They make it plain, if it was not before, that in his suffering and death on the cross, not in his becoming flesh, the Son of God offered the ultimate proof of his obedience. This adds up to the theology of the suffering Son of Man, a doctrine that is hardly found outside the Synoptic Gospels.

The "therefore" of v. 9 is temporal and consequential, but it expresses no inevitable connection between the act of Christ's obedience and the ensuing act of God glorifying him. The RSV's choice of a verb to translate the Greek *echarisato* is not too fortunate in this case. God has "bestowed" on Christ the name of Lord, yes, but far more importantly, he has "graced" him with this name. We have here no quid pro quo but the grace of God by which he exalts the humble, truly an example for the Philippians.

We cannot be sure by what route—if there was a single route—the New Testament church came to call upon its resurrected Savior by the title *kyrios,* Lord. It was a title current in the Greek-speaking world into which the church was born. It was a title assumed by kings and caesars, as was the title "Savior," for that matter. The title already connoted divinity, in those times when kings and caesars were too often counted as gods. But it was also the title under which Jews and the Jewish church had long known the God of Israel's salvation, and it is difficult to imagine that this usage had nothing to do with the church's choice of this word to acknowledge the continued presence of the saving Christ in their midst. It is particularly difficult when we consider this present passage, which explicitly applies to Christ the words of Isa. 45:23, originally spoken of Israel's God and Savior (cf. Isa. 45:21): "To me every knee shall bow, every tongue shall confess."

In becoming Lord of the church Christ did not merely regain the "form" (*morphē,* condition, state) of God of which he "emptied himself" in the incarnation. Rather, he was exalted *above* the static condition of being "merely" a God to that of being a saving, acting God—a saving, acting God, moreover, whose exaltation exceeds even that described in Isaiah 45, since it extends not only over all the nations of the earth but also over every creature "in heaven and on earth and under the earth."

We have had occasion before to observe that in biblical religion relatively little interest is shown in divine attributes in the abstract, simply as matters of theoretical speculation. For biblical religion the qualities of God that count are those that have been revealed in his relations with humankind. In turn, these qualities so revealed in the historical experience of humankind are the only means whereby it has been given to human beings truly to "know" God—to know him, and not merely to imagine him. The title Lord proclaims Jesus God *and*

Savior, even as Israel before had known its God precisely as he was its Savior. And now, because of God's ultimate revelation of himself in Christ, it is only through the confession of the lordship of Jesus Christ that glory can be given to God the Father.

GOSPEL: LUKE 2:21

This single verse is set by Luke in the context of Jesus' circumcision, eight days after his birth, in keeping with the prescription of Lev. 12:3. It is at this time that he came "under the law." (Gal. 4:4 has him "born under the law," but it is not hard to imagine why Paul, conscious of the Galatians' proclivities, did not mention the circumcision of Jesus.) On this occasion for the first time he would be publicly called by the name "given by the angel before he was conceived in the womb" (Luke 1:21, 31). In Matthew's version of the birth and infancy narrative, we will remember, the name of Jesus was also made known by an angelic messenger, but to Joseph, and after Mary's pregnancy had become evident (Matt. 1:21). Both Matthew and Luke have seen significance in the fact that this name, despite its common currency in Jesus' time, had the meaning "savior." (Actually, at least in its full form, it meant "Yahweh is savior." But this had probably been forgotten in the general disuse of the name Yahweh.)

There is no ambivalence in the liturgical tradition responsible for our celebrating both "Jesus" and "Lord" under the one rubric of our Savior's holy Name. Both names are of equal importance. Luke evidently intends in this verse that "Jesus," unmentioned since 1:31, should come as a climactic utterance, despite his having already named Jesus as "Lord" in 2:11.

For one thing, "Jesus" is the name of a historical person, a person whose existence upon this earth at a given era in human history is, theoretically at least, as verifiable as that of Herod Antipas or Pontius Pilate or any other of the historical persons who appear in the New Testament. It may be very true, as some like to maintain, that the "quest for the historical Jesus," whether it is the "old" or the "new" quest, is a chimera, that even if successful it could add nothing to the Christ of faith as he is presented to us in the Gospels, that if anything it might detract from that presentation and interfere with it. Possibly true, but not to the point. The point is that when the Gospels present us with the Christ of faith they are presenting a historical Savior.

The kerygma of the Gospels is an interpreted history, as all history is, but it is the kerygma of a person and not merely of a symbol. A person who lived and suffered, hungered and thirsted, died and was buried, before ever he took on the symbolism of Last Adam, Redeemer, or Lord. Veneration of the name of the historical Jesus of Nazareth is our safeguard against Gnosticism and Docetism, heresies which diluted or denied the humanity of Christ and thus the reality of the redemption long before it occurred to later Christians to question the divinity of their Savior.

"Jesus" and "Lord" are of equal importance; without either one, the other could not have meaning for us. Had there been no Jesus, obviously there could not have been, in the divine economy, a kerygmatic Lord of the church. But also, a Jesus of Nazareth who was never constituted Lord would be equally meaningless for us, another cipher among many in the complex history of religions. Philippians summed it up, as does Rom. 1:1–7, the alternate second reading for today: Jesus Christ is Lord!

The Second Sunday After Christmas

Lutheran	Roman Catholic	Episcopal	Pres/UCC/Chr	Meth/COCU
Isa. 61:10—62:3	Sir. 24:1–4, 8–12	Jer. 31:7–14	Prov. 8:22–31	Isa. 61:10—62:3 or Sir. 24:1–2, 8–12
Eph. 1:3–6, 15–18	Eph. 1:3–6, 15–18	Eph. 1:3–6, 15–19a	Eph. 1:15–23	Eph. 1:3–6, 15–23
John 1:1–18	John 1:1–18 or John 1:1–5, 9–14	Matt. 2:13–15, 19–23 or Luke 2:41–52 or Matt. 2:1–12	John 1:1–5, 9–14	Matt. 2:13–15, 19–23

FIRST LESSON: ISAIAH 61:10—62:3

There is a subdued kind of triumphalism that pervades today's readings, appropriate to the conclusion of this season of anticipation and accomplishment during which marvelous events have been commemorated and relived.

In this Isaian passage the lectionary has actually combined one of the biblical author's poems with part of another. However, there is a basic unity of thought that binds the two together, and all the verses jointly combine to produce a hymn of thanksgiving that is entirely appropriate to the occasion. The poems are part of a complex (Isaiah 60—62) that is the product of a postexilic Jewish community in interesting parallel with the post-Resurrection community of early Christianity that produced the New Testament writings. Like the Christians of the New Testament, this community newly reestablished in Jerusalem had seen the beginning of a promised salvation whose consummation, however, was strangely delayed, or so they thought. Isaiah 60—62 were written to reassure and to console, to recall the Lord's promises, and to repeat them with such confidence in their fulfillment that the community can be invited to rejoice in them as though they were already accomplished. It is not surprising that in Luke 4:18–19 Jesus reads from Isa. 61:1–2 to announce the beginning of the messianic age.

In the first part of the lectionary passage we hear Jerusalem speaking, the restored and redeemed Jerusalem of prophetic vision rejoicing in the Lord's salvation. The following and concluding verses which complement and confirm Jerusalem's praise seem to be those of the prophetic figure who is responsible for this poetic complex, one who was a disciple and imitator of the Second Isaiah of the Servant Songs.

Jerusalem begins to speak in words that remind us of the Magnificat, Mary's prayer of humble thanksgiving according to Luke 1:46–55. This resemblance is hardly accidental. The redeemed or "glorified" Jerusalem, recipient of the salvation and the righteousness that comes from God, is a personification of God's redeemed people, like the heavenly Jerusalem of Rev. 21:9—22:5. In turn, as we have remarked before, both in the Johannine literature of the New Testament and in Luke, Mary the mother of the Messiah often appears in the guise of the female figure representing the church. In one metaphor, the church is the Bride of Christ, continuing a symbolism that began with the prophet Hosea and is found in this Isaian passage, but in another metaphor the church is she who gives birth to the Christ of universal salvation (the woman of Rev. 12:1–6), by the proclamation of the good news to all the nations of the earth.

Jerusalem rejoices as a bride adorned for her husband: the New

Testament parallel is Rev. 21:2. The parallel is more than verbal, for the historical situation is the same. The festal garments of the holy city are salvation and righteousness, corresponding with the jewels worn by a bride on her wedding day. It is proper that the simile should include the garland gracing the brow of a bridegroom on the same occasion, for in glorifying Jerusalem the Lord glorifies himself. Also, the bridal clothing of salvation and righteousness are gifts of the Lord, his before they are hers. Righteousness (alternatively, "justice") is both the quality of God that prompts him to be just to himself, to show mercy to those to whom he has pledged himself, and the quality with which he endows those on whom he showers his favors. The thought, again, was first Hosea's: "I will betroth you to me for ever; I will betroth you to me in righteousness and in justice, in steadfast love, and in mercy. I will betroth you to me in faithfulness; and you shall know the Lord" (Hos. 2:19–20).

In v. 11 the metaphor changes, from a bridal scene to another favorite Palestinian motif, that of the fabled productivity of the soil that could hardly be expected except in an eschatological future. In truth, however, the two verses are more intimately connected than one might suppose. Fertility, after all, is in the biblical perspective not only the desired end but even the creational design in the bringing together of man and woman (Gen. 1:28; cf. also Ruth 4:11–12). The boldness of Hosea in first using the marriage metaphor to symbolize God's covenantal relationship with Israel consisted precisely in the fact that in Palestine fertility religions were endemic—nature religions that encouraged sexual promiscuity as the means of guaranteeing the productivity of "the grain, the wine, and the oil" (Hos. 2:8) vital to the survival of an agricultural people. Hosea added to the metaphor the essential Israelite ingredient of marital fidelity, and that ingredient is reflected in our Isaian text. The marital union of God with Jerusalem "will cause righteousness and praise to spring forth before all the nations." Righteousness, still both the act and the gift of God, will burgeon in Israel and in the world of nations. Praise, the sacred *tehillah* of Israel's worship, will echo from the Gentiles (cf. Mal. 1:11).

In 62:1–3 the prophet acclaims the redeemed Jerusalem that is to be, the Jerusalem that has been speaking in the preceding verses. His praise is a reiteration of the poetry of Isaiah 60 and is paralleled by the exuberant eulogy that burst forth from the lips of another postexilic prophet, which is to be read in Zech. 8:1–8, 20–23. (By RSV this latter passage is considered to be prose, but other versions and editions of the Bible regard it as mostly poetry.) Since the poet's words are both prayer and prophecy, his praise is intended also to hasten the day of final vindication and salvation. At that glorious time, with all the nations and kings of the earth witness to her queenly estate, Jerusalem shall be called by a new name. So also Ezekiel (48:35) had said, calling her Yahweh-shammah: "The Lord is there." The New Testament was to know yet other names, "which the mouth of the Lord will give."

Our Old Testament readings for this season thus conclude on the same note with which they began on the First Sunday in Advent. We are left with a vision of a coming salvation from Israel's God which will somehow encompass all who live on earth—a salvation and redemption awaiting fulfillment.

SECOND LESSON: EPHESIANS 1:3–6, 15–18

Part of that fulfillment of which we spoke above is to be found celebrated here in these verses from the Epistle to the Ephesians. This lectionary selection again seems to be a composite of sorts. Ephesians 1:3–14 is a hymn, apparently a baptismal hymn in the manner of 1 Pet. 1:3–12, which the Pauline author of Ephesians, whether it was Paul himself or someone who wrote in the person of Paul, made into the introductory part of his letter. Of this hymn, vv. 3–6 represent the first two strophes out of six. The concluding vv. 15–18 of the lectionary reading, on the other hand, are the words of the author of the epistle, taking up from the hymn and incorporating it into his writing.

Since the material is so closely related in thought, there is no hindrance to its exposition as a whole. However, there is some added value to the recognition that we do have here a hymn, a piece of ancient Christian liturgy. The vocabulary and some of the constructions found in Eph. 1:3–14 have often been the despair of Greek scholars, grappling with phrases originally meant to be sung rather than analyzed, as one commentator has put it. All that we know about the liturgical life of primitive Christianity we have to surmise from vague descriptions like those of Paul in 1 Corinthians or Luke in the Acts of the Apostles, from allusions to the "psalms and hymns and spiritual songs" of Col. 3:16 and Eph. 5:19, from what look like liturgical fragments which a New Testament author found it opportune to cite (perhaps Eph. 5:14, for example), and, finally, from integral hymns such as this one and, perhaps, some of those in the Revelation of John which would seem to have had no other accountable origin if not the liturgy. These verses, therefore, should be precious to us, and not merely as bits of historical data. As they form part of our liturgy, they join us to the worship of our ancestors in the faith.

The epistolary conventions of the time called for a blessing or a thanksgiving after the initial salutation. By introducing the liturgical hymn into his letter, the Pauline author has achieved the result of combining the two, since the hymn is throughout a blessing or praise of God and, as vv. 15–16 make clear, it is also a blessing that calls forth thanksgiving.

God is blessed precisely because he is the God and Father of our Lord Jesus Christ and because it is in Christ that he has blessed us. The blessings he has bestowed on us are spiritual: not merely as distinguished from the material, but as pertaining to the order of the spirit, as transporting us from this world of the flesh into the *epourania,* "the heavenly places." In union with Christ, because of what God has done in Christ, we inhabit a new sphere of existence. We inhabit that sphere of existence in the church. It can be called heavenly because it is that of Christ glorified, at the right hand of God (cf. v. 20). Thus the predestination of which v. 4 speaks, God's choice of us from all eternity, is not yet an election to glory but rather an election to grace. This is made even plainer when the text goes on to say that God chose us in Christ, that we might stand before him holy and blameless. The commentary and parallel to this verse appears in v. 7 of the hymn that is not in our reading: our election was to redemption through the blood of Christ, the forgiveness of sins.

"Holy" and "blameless" were originally purely formal terms, even negative in meaning, and are sometimes so used even today. (The word RSV translates "blameless," *amōmos,* in the Septuagint is ordinarily used of a person or a thing that is ritually acceptable.) Obviously in this context they are anything but formal and negative. God's election has also imposed on us the duty to lead lives worthy of his call. The duty is consequent on the call, which was motivated only by God's love for us.

God has predestined us in love to be his sons, literally, "to adoptive sonship." This term, found only in the Pauline literature of the New Testament, is sometimes employed by Paul eschatologically (as in Rom. 8:19), but also, as it is here, of the present state of Christians (so in Gal. 3:26, for example). While "sons" or, perhaps, "children of God" may be the most idiomatic way of putting the text into English, it is well to bear in mind that it is a collective noun that is so rendered. That is to say, we are not being encouraged to think of our relationship either to God or to Christ in any purely personal or private way. We are brought into the heavenly sphere and declared God's very dear children in Christ not as individuals but as the members of a church of believers. Like Israel of old, we are saved as a people, or we are not saved at all.

This point is given confirmation of a sort in the next verse, where yet again the gratuity of God's grace is stressed, bestowed on us in "the Beloved" (v. 6). "The Beloved," a christological title much favored in the postapostolic church, particularly in literature that had kept contact with the Semitic origins of Christianity *(The Epistle of Barnabas, The Shepherd of Hermas, 1 Clement),* was the Septuagint translation of the Jeshurun of Isa. 44:2, the messianic title the Second Isaiah gave to Israel as the personified Servant of the Lord's redemption.

The exhortations of vv. 15–18 which follow the hymn are delicately concealed in an act of thanksgiving for the faith and love that the author professes have already been shown by those who have accepted God's call. Theirs is an election of hope, they who have been called by the God of glory. What is now needed is lives lived in accordance with that hope and in full awareness of the realities to which it beckons. "Having the eyes of your hearts enlightened" is an expression rich in Semitisms. It has nothing to do, of course, with mere intellectual appreciation. The heart is, biblically, the center of one's inner existence, the seat of conviction out of which come action and practice. "The fool says in his heart, 'There is no God' " (Ps. 14:1; Ps. 53:1)—and acts as though there were none. The enlightenment of which our author speaks, the spirit of wisdom and of revelation in the knowledge of God and of what is the inheritance to which we have been invited (v. 18)—these are to be had only through perseverance in the faith, hope, and charity which, we will recall (Rom. 13:12), are our armor of light. Only by doing do we learn what we must do. Only by experiencing the taste that God has given us of his love can we appreciate what that love has finally destined for us and why we must have it.

As Christmas is to Easter, as promise is to realization, so is rejoicing in God's grace to our perseverance in it. Now we end this Christmas season as we ought, praising God and thanking him for the gift of Christ and for destining us to share in his gift. We thank God for our Christian calling. But we are reminded that the only adequate praise and thanks that we can give to God is our continued openness to his grace and to its ultimate workings, whatever they may be.

GOSPEL: JOHN 1:1–18

Our final Gospel portion assigned in the readings for this season is, once more, one of those passages so familiar to every Christian that commentary seems superfluous and almost an impertinence. It is the New Testament passage that, above all, doubtless reaches the high-water mark attained by its christology "from above," its so-called high christology which is deductive rather than inductive. In it Jesus Christ, whose name and title are not mentioned until v. 17, and whose unique sonship is only hinted at in v. 14 and explicitly affirmed only at the very end, in v. 18, is throughout characterized as the Word of God, that is, his utterance, his emanation. This theology of Christ the Word of God from all eternity, one with God and God indeed, the very cause and rationale of all creation, has become a given for all orthodox Christianity. Yet it is unique, just as the Gospel of John itself is unique.

Pratically every single theological statement made by or about the Christ of the church's faith in the Fourth Gospel is anticipated in this prologue. He is the light of God's enlightenment come into the world (9:5), he is the way to God, God's truth and life made manifest through his coming (14:6), the ultimate revelation of God become visible in the flesh of a perfect human being, embodying that "grace and truth" (*ḥesed,* steadfast love, and *emeth,* fidelity) which is virtually an Old Testament definition of God (Exod. 34:6, for example). The Old Testament (the Moses of v. 17) did mediate a vision of the God of grace and truth (though John is probably thinking of Exod. 33:20–23), but by comparison it was a clouded vision. The law, the Old Testament revelation, did not have its end in itself. As Paul would say (Gal 3:24), the law was a custodian, a *paidogōgos,* one who leads a child by the hand, waiting upon but never wholly anticipating the new thing that has been brought by God in Christ.

One line in this passage requires special comment, in accord with some of the thoughts we have gathered from other scriptural readings of this season and to underscore one of the chief theological assertions we have found in them.

The RSV margin to vv. 3b–4a offers an alternate reading—it is really a question of the correct punctuation of the Greek text—that probably should be accepted, as it has been by other modern English versions of the New Testament (e.g., NEB, NAB, Goodspeed, Jerusalem Bible, Good News Bible). In the first place, the existing RSV, "without him was not anything made that was made," seems to make for a rather tiresome pleonasm that is remarkable even in the Gospel of John, where repetitiveness is part of the style. But more importantly, the woodenness of this translation may obscure a very important christological point intended by the evangelist.

We should read, therefore, with the RSV margin (and with the best of the ancient manuscripts and the testimony of the early church fathers): "That which has been made was life in him." Or, more simply and literally with the Greek: "What came to be in him was life, and the life was the light of men." Once again we are being told, even in a writing as profound in theological thought as this one is, that we are reading the words of a Gospel and not of a dogmatic treatise on God the Creator. The life about which John the evangelist is speaking is, above all, eternal life, which is a gift that God holds in store for those who love him. Eternal life is not ours by nature, in virtue of our creation. It is, or the possibility of it is, something *made* for us, and ours only in virtue of a new creation *in Christ*. Christ the eternal Word of God is not, by that fact alone, our Savior. Our Savior is Christ the Word of God sent by God into the world and endowed by him with that which has constituted Christ a life-giving spirit (1 Cor. 15:45), the breath of new and everlasting life.

If we would truly comprehend the meaning of the season we have once more relived and put the celebration of our Lord's nativity in its proper scriptural perspective, we should have a better recognition of its relation to the greater mysteries of the Christian faith. One other "mind" should have become ours in Christ Jesus, just as it was his mind when the eternal Word of God became flesh and reckoned that equality with God was not a thing to be clung to in sterile embrace but rather to be divested of (Phil. 2:6), so that he might assume the role of servant to become our Savior.

Another thought should occur to us before we take leave of this prologue to John's Gospel. In v. 11, the RSV reads: "He came to his own home, and his own people received him not." The translation, while perfectly justifiable, is a trifle free. The English Bible of which

RSV is a revision had, word for word with the Greek: "He came unto his own, and his own received him not." But in either case, whether or not we supply the words "home" and "people," we ought not too hastily conclude, as some do, that by "home" is meant Judea and by "people" simply the Jews. John does mean this, no doubt, but not only this. Historically Jesus' mission was, for all practical purposes, confined to Jews, and when Jesus was rejected he was rejected by Jews. However, John's Gospel was not written for archival interest; and while the evangelist is always capable of addressing several levels of meaning at the same time, he does not bring in the incarnation, and thus the earthly life of the Word who became Jesus Christ, until v. 14.

And so John must have in mind also the entire course of time in which the Word of God has fallen on the deaf ears of the people to whom it has been sent. Nor may this course of time be restricted to that of the people of Israel whose history was indeed, in prophetic eyes, one of resistance to God's Word. Rather, as the parallel v. 10 indicates, it is the history of the world of which John speaks: it is the world that knew him not. And the world remains. For John the "world" is unbelief. It is a world to which Christians do not properly belong, but which they must inhibit, and to whose allurements they are always prone.

Through belief in the Word we have been given the power to become children of God, through a new birth. "But we have this treasure in earthen vessels" (2 Cor. 4:7). Our reading of John's glorious prologue should encourage in us no feelings of complacency as we daily strive to give a proper home to the Word and to the grace and truth that have come to us through Jesus Christ.